KV-746-731

THE JARGON OF THE PROFESSIONS

By the same author

The Businessman in Public
The Dictionary of Diseased English
The End of Gin and Tonic Man: a Future for Public Relations

THE JARGON OF THE PROFESSIONS

KENNETH HUDSON

First published 1978 by
THE MACMILLAN PRESS LTD
London and Basingstoke
Associated companies in Delhi
Dublin Hong Kong Johannesburg Lagos
Melbourne New York Singapore Tokyo

British Library Cataloguing in Publication Data

Hudson, Kenneth
The jargon of the professions.
1. English language – Jargon
I. Title
427'.09 PE1449

ISBN 0-333-21437-4

Printed in Great Britain by
BILLING & SONS LTD
Guildford Worcester and London

Contents

Introduction: the Meaning of 'Jargon' and of 'the Professions'

Technical language is not, in itself, jargon, and it is not a criminal or moral offence to write or speak in a way which is not immediately understood by the man in the street. Every profession necessarily has its own terminology, without which its members cannot think or express themselves. To deprive them of such words would be to condemn them to inactivity. If one wished to kill a profession, to remove its cohesion and its strength, the most effective way would be to forbid the use of its characteristic language.

On the other hand, there are people, possibly many people, whose supposedly technical language does not stand up to close examination. It is bogus, existing only to impress the innocent and unwary, and interfering with the process of communication instead of improving it. It may well suggest this profession, rather than that, and it may, in small doses, have a certain exotic charm, provided one is in the mood to accept and enjoy it. But it is not essential, cannot be justified on practical grounds and fulfils no purpose, except possibly to act as a kind of masonic glue between different members of the same profession. The solidarity-value of such nonsense-language certainly should not be underestimated.

Thirty years ago, Sir Ernest Gowers, the great crusader against linguistic nonsense in the public service, attempted to define 'jargon' in a way that would allow it to be easily distinguished from technicality.

> The proper meaning of 'jargon' [he wrote] is writing that employs technical words not commonly intelligible. 'Catachresis' for instance is grammarians' jargon for using a word in a wrong sense. When grammarians call writing jargon merely because it is verbose, circumlocutory and flabby, they themselves commit the sin of catachresis that they denounce in others.[1]

In the successor to *Plain Words, ABC of Plain Words,* Sir Ernest pursues the matter a little further.

> A dictionary definition of jargon [he reminds us] is a word applied

> contemptuously to the language of scholars, the terminology of a science or art, or the cant of a class, sect, trade or profession. When it was confined to that sense, it was a useful word. But it has been handled so promiscuously of recent years that the edge has been taken off it, and now, as has been well said, it signifies little more than any speech that a person feels to be inferior to his own.
>
> When officials are accused of writing jargon, what is usually meant is that they affect a pompous and flabby verbosity. The Americans have a pleasant word for it – 'gobbledygook'. It cannot be questioned that there is too much of that sort of thing in the general run of present-day writing, both official and other. . . . But there is also a jargon in the strict sense of the word, and official writing is not free from it. Technical terms are used – especially conventional phrases invented by a government department – which are understood inside the department, but are unintelligible to outsiders. That is true jargon.

Sir Ernest then proceeds to illustrate his point with the beginning of a Civil Service circular: 'The physical progressing of building cases should be confined to . . .' and comments:

> Nobody could say what meaning this was intended to convey unless he held the key. It is not English, except in the sense that the words are English words. They are a group of symbols used in conventional sense known only to the parties to the convention. It may be said that no harm is done, because the instruction is not meant to be read by anyone unfamiliar with the departmental jargon. But using jargon is a dangerous habit; it is easy to forget that the public do not understand it, and to slip into the use of it in explaining things to them.[2]

More recently, Peter Wright has attempted to establish a distinction between jargon and slang. 'Jargon,' he decides, 'the specialised technical language of different occupations and interests, is fundamentally impersonal and serious, whilst slang is basically friendly and humorous. To the layman a chemical equation, and to consumers advertisements for products, including 'ingredients X, Y and Z', are meaningless jargon.'[3]

Sir Ernest Gowers was writing thirty years ago, before the real rise to power of the most influential and culpable jargon-makers in the English language, the psychologists and sociologists and the management experts. He also strangely, but perhaps wisely, decided to ignore the flood of jargon produced by politicians, especially on the far Left. His chief and very beneficial concern was with the language of Civil Servants.

The time may now have come, however, for the meaning of 'jargon' to move on a further stage, in the way it has been doing for more than five hundred years. Used precisely and with present-day conditions in mind, it is a word which could help us to identify society's enemies more closely. It could indicate intention and effect, as well as characteristics.

With these possibilities in mind, one might suggest that jargon, in the last quarter of the twentieth century, contains four essential elements:

1. It reflects a particular profession or occupation.
2. It is pretentious, with only a small kernel of meaning underneath it.
3. It is used mainly by intellectually inferior people, who feel a need to convince the general public of their importance.
4. It is, deliberately or accidentally, mystifying.

The best minds in any profession are never guilty of jargon, except when they are very tired. Pedestrian minds are drawn towards it automatically and to the most frightening extent. Jargon, one could suggest, is the natural weapon of highly paid people with very little of any value to say. It is a sad and ironical comment on our society that many people feel released from the pressure to use jargon only when they have reached the top of their profession, by which time it may be too late to change one's habits, however much one might wish to. Ambitious people, still busy climbing the ladder, may well consider it professionally dangerous to use straightforward language. One therefore has the paradox that only the person who has finally arrived, with his reputation secure, can afford to be simple and jargon-free. Lesser mortals appear to need their jargon, as a membership-badge of their profession. They do not have the confidence to face the world without it.

There is always the possibility, alas, that people use jargon because they have never learnt or been taught to write properly. At a discussion which took place in Cambridge in 1958, Dr C. F. A. Pantin spoke with some feeling on the point, as editor of a scientific periodical.

> The most important part of my editorial work [he said] consists of trying to help contributors to say clearly and concisely what they have to say. Many Universities encourage the production of long-winded theses for the degree of Doctor of Philosophy. All too often it is left to the editors to show the contributor how to winnow this stuff and to extract from it the lucid and cogent statement of fact and argument that is worth publication. Nor is this difficulty confined to the young. I have yet to attend an international conference which did not illustrate how firmly men and women believe, perhaps correctly, that professional advancement is closely knit with long-winded and excessive publication, particularly in the highly specialised fields of learning.[4]

Editors can, however, exercise a pressure different from, and much less beneficial than that suggested by Dr Pantin, especially nowadays when all forms of publication are expensive. In their anxiety to save space, they may well encourage the German-type double and triple adjectives and the absence of prepositions which produce such over-compressed and disagreeable-sounding prose.

No professional publication contains less jargon, in our sense of the term, than the *British Medical Journal.* What there is is usually very mild, of the 'ambulant patient' type. Two generations of editors have conducted a vigorous compaign against it and the results are there to be seen in any issue one cares to select. Some editorial blue-pencilling is still carried out, but a quarter of a century of campaigning and of rejection of potential contributions has had its effect. Once it becomes generally known that the well-written article is likely to be published and the badly-written one sent back, an improvement in style is almost inevitable.

One cannot say the same about a number of the journals devoted to psychiatry and psychology, especially in the United States. *Archives of General Psychiatry*, Chicago, for instance, is full of dreadful stuff, of which one example will be, for the moment, more than sufficient.

> Other group modalities often used with children are play, behavior modification, and the verbal approach . . . . Play materials are selected to evoke group members' expression and resolution of personal conflicts. Therapeutic ingredients are the therapist-child relationship and therapist clarification – interpretation of feelings expressed through the child's play. Member-to-member interaction is seen as less important in play than in activity-group treatment. In behavior modification groups, the armentarium of behavioral techniques is applied. Treatment goals are limited to the modification of specific behavior patterns. The verbal group therapies include client-centered counseling and insight oriented psychotherapy. Definitive features of these modalities are discussion of the patients' problems and mobilization of member-to-member and member-to-therapist interaction to improve psychobehavioral functioning.[5]

The key test for jargon is the question: 'Could this have been expressed more simply without communication suffering in the process?' If the answer is 'Yes', then the probability is that one is faced with a piece of jargon. The passage just quoted from *Archives of General Psychiatry* contains a good deal of jargon, measured by this standard. The following, from the same journal, is not jargon, however.

> If concomitant antiparkinson medication is required, it may have to be continued after HALDOL haloperidol is discontinued, because of the difference in excretion rates. If both are discontinued simultaneously, extrapyramidal symptoms may occur. Intraocular pressure may increase

when antichlorinergic drugs, including antiparkinson agents, are administered concomitantly with HALDOL haloperidol.[6]

This is technical medical language, a professional code which is perfectly intelligible to anyone who has learnt its elements and who knows how to interpret them. The information cannot be translated into anything simpler.

It is important, however, to distinguish different levels of technicality. One can easily illustrate this from the medical field. An example of high-technicality language, which is not jargon, is:

> Normal women had higher mean (this is gamma) γ-globulin levels than males. There was evidence of connective-tissue disease in 10% of female relatives of patients with systemic lupus erythematosus. A bimodal distribution of serum γ-globulin levels and a raised incidence of antinuclear factor was found in relatives of patients with systemic lupus erythematosus. Rheumatoid factor was slightly more common in female relatives of patients with systemic lupus than would be expected. In addition to familial factors, environmental factors such as hyrallazine therapy might be important in systemic lupus erythematosus.[7]

This is medium-technicality language:

> Eczema and other common skin conditions, whether wet or dry, usually respond rapidly to treatment with 'Hydroderm' ointment. It provides the anti-inflammatory, anti-allergic and antipruritic actions of hydrocortisone; and the anti-bacterial cover of neomycin and bacitiacin, which are effective against most common skin pathogens.[8]

Low-technicality language has a different flavour and texture:

> Depression becomes more common with advancing age and is all too often overlooked as a diagnosis. This is an important omission, as effective treatment is possible. The diagnosis may be overlooked, because an elderly person, particularly one with physical illness or disability, may be regarded as having sufficient circumstances in his life situation to account for the observed happiness or pessimism. In other patients hypochondriacal symptoms may throw the emphasis on to physical disease, so that the mental diagnosis is missed. Alternatively, very severe depression with withdrawal and apathy may be mistaken for dementia. Many depressed old people may remain unrecognised because they put on a brave front for the doctor and appear cheerful superficially, but specific questioning about mood, appetite and sleep may show the true state of affairs.[9]

One finds three kinds of defence of professional jargon, especially of the jargon and near-jargon employed by doctors, lawyers and economists. Such language is said to be more condensed and therefore time-saving; morale-raising and supportive, in that it allows one professional to recognise another without waste of time; and, often though but rarely expressed, an indispensable means of keeping the public at a respectful distance. The last argument, however, is wearing rather thin, as education spreads. In Western society, the expert no longer has the priestly function he once possessed. He is required to justify his privileged position. The magic of jargon has lost much of its power.

The doctors especially are coming to recognise this, although it would be an exaggeration to say that they no longer display the characteristics of a caste. Their rarity value still makes it possible to behave as if they are not as other men. Medical arrogance is still, alas, very much with us. But there are welcome signs that it may be decreasing. It is certainly under attack.

The well-known heretic, Dr Thomas Szasz, has been waging all-out war against medical obscurantism and jargon for many years, and has made both friends and enemies in the process.

> I propose [he writes] a medical reformation analogous to the Protestant Reformation, specifically a 'protest' against the systematic mystification of man's relationship to his body to give the layman direct access to the language and contents of the pharmacopoeia. It is significant that until recently physicians wrote prescriptions in Latin and that medical diagnoses are still couched in a jargon whose chief aim is to awe and mystify the laity. Were man to have unencumbered access to his own body and the means of chemically altering it, it would spell the end of Medicine, at least as we now know it. This is why, with faith in Scientific Medicine so strong, there is little interest in this kind of medical reform; physicians fear the loss of their privileges; laymen the loss of their protections.[10]

What Dr Szasz is saying is that the less patients, or some patients, understand medical language, the more they respect the power of those who use it. Magic is a necessary part of treatment, and doctors, he believes, take good care to encourage such an attitude. The jargon, so to speak, is the cure, and doctors have indeed been able to earn a handsome living by language designed to 'awe and mystify the laity'. But the laity is not quite as passive or as ignorant now as it was fifty years ago. The great days of medical jargon may be coming to an end and the revolution for which Dr Szasz has been longing could be closer than he thinks.

He is certainly not the only doctor to see a need for radical change. Dr Mae McMillan, of Houston, for instance, believes that 'a major communications gap' between doctor and patient has got to be closed. 'Although we psychiatrists feel that we have a valid and usable body of facts about behavior and personality development,' she observes, 'the layman feels that much of what we say is speculation. Psychiatrists and other members of the mental health disciplines must assume responsibility for this impression. Our sense of responsibility to disseminate information about human motivation and behavior should also carry over in our making it comprehensible.'[11]

Dr McMillan is perhaps being a little too kind to her profession. What many laymen feel about the way psychiatrists talk and write is not that it is mere speculation but that much of it is empty nonsense which has gone unchallenged too long. Once this stage of disbelief and suspicion has been reached, psychiatrists are indeed well advised to devote time to explaining what it is that they are about.

But in this demand for explanation and justification one can go too far. 'Every profession,' as a pioneering survey of nearly half a century ago pointed out, 'lives in a world of its own. The language which is spoken by the inhabitants, the landmarks so familiar to them, their customs and conventions can only be thoroughly learnt by those who reside there.'[12]

But what is a profession? In their 1933 analysis, Carr-Saunders and Wilson distinguished twenty-nine occupations, or groups of occupations, which seemed to them worthy to be called professions. With most there can be no quarrel, but one or two of their choices, such as 'brokers' and 'biophysical assistants' may cause eyebrows to be raised. They omitted, somewhat whimsically, the Church and the Army.

> The former is left out because all those functions related to the ordinary business of life, education among them, which used to fall to the Church are spiritual, and we are only concerned with the professions in their relation to the ordinary business of life. The army is omitted, because the service which soldiers are trained to render is one which it is hoped they will never be called upon to perform.[13]

The authors of *The Professions* dodged the difficult task of defining a profession.

'It is no part of our purpose [they wrote] to attempt to draw a line between professions and other vocations; we are not concerned to say what vocations are professions and what are not. We are therefore absolved from the necessity of examining all those vocations which claim professional rank in order that we may decide upon their true position. Indeed, the drawing of a boundary-line would be an arbitrary procedure, and we shall not offer, either now or later, a definition of professionalism. Nevertheless, when we have completed our survey, it will emerge that the typical profession exhibits a complex of characteristics, and that other vocations approach this condition more or less closely, owing to the possession of some of these characteristics fully or partially developed.'[14]

This amounts to saying that although 'profession' cannot be defined, it is possible to recognise a profession by its 'complex of characteristics'. Grasping the nettle, we may suggest that, in order to be recognised as a profession, an occupation, or, to use the more elevated word, a vocation, has to satisfy these requirements:

1. Entry to it – that is, full membership – must be permitted only to those who have satisfied an examining and supervisory body that they have reached a satisfactory standard of training. There will be a document issued to successful candidates, which makes this clear and a register of the members of the profession will be maintained by the governing body.
2. Continued membership of the profession must be conditional on observing certain clearly understood conditions of behaviour and competence.
3. Removal from the register of anyone who is judged unfit to practise must be under the direct control of the professional body itself, not of the courts.

One can construct without difficulty a list of occupations which meet these requirements. It would include doctors, dentists, lawyers, nurses, pharmacists and actuaries. It would not include teachers, architects, actors, journalists and engineers, however often one may talk of 'the profession of journalism' or refer to an actor as 'a true professional'. Anyone, at least in Britain, is free to work as a teacher, a journalist or an architect. Regrettably and, as some may think, scandalously, he is not obliged to have undergone any approved course of training or to possess any certificate of competeence. In some instances, journalism and acting being excellent examples, permission to work is conditional on trade union membership, not on any form of paper qualification.

The legal protection given to different occupations varies a great deal, and in subtle ways. With doctors and pharmacists the position is perfectly clear. No-one may either call himself a doctor or a pharmacist or carry out such work without possessing approved qualifications and being registered. Anyone, however, may carry out architectural work provided he makes no attempt to describe himself as an architect.

Teachers may think of themselves as a profession, and frequently describe themselves as belonging to one. The press may flatter them by following their example in the matter. In a leading article headed 'Uneasy and Unsure Teachers',[15] *The Times* can say, for example 'The teachers have recently suffered three blows, any one of which would have caused ruffled professional feelings'; 'Teacher training colleges are having to close and the profession is having to come to terms with a period of rapid growth and keen demand for its services'; and, concerning the Secretary for Education, 'The conference seemed if anything relieved at her forthrightness and her emphasis on discussing ways of doing it with the profession.'

Both *The Times* and the Secretary could, however, use the word 'profession' a thousand times without altering in the slightest the fact that anyone in Britain, qualifications or no qualifications, is entirely free to work as a teacher and to describe himself as a teacher.

Certain occupations are understandably anxious to be considered professions, in order to achieve at least a veneer of respectability and to improve their status. It is only fair to point out that some of these have been trying hard for years to prevent the employment of unqualified people and to set up for themselves a governing and examining body similar to that which exists for lawyers and doctors. School-teaching and museum work are cases in point. But there is a difference between wanting something and getting it, and however much teachers and museum curators may talk of 'the teaching profession' and 'the museum profession', the fact remains that in the strict sense of the term these are not as yet professions and quite possibly never will be. There is, in Britain, no such person as a licensed teacher, any more than there is a licensed museums practitioner. Doctors, on the other hand, have a piece of paper which tells the world that they are qualified and licensed to practise medicine, and that is the end of the matter. Lawyers are in the same position. Anyone who attempts to work as a doctor or a lawyer without possessing such a piece of paper is likely to find himself in serious legal trouble and may well go to prison for his attempt to deceive the public.

What this amounts to is that governments have acknowledged the need to protect the community against unqualified doctors and lawyers, but that they have not so far been convinced that unqualified builders, teachers, engineers or journalists are an equal menace. Regrettably, one has to admit that the possession of a certificate which announces to the world that in 1947 a man was adjudged to be a competent doctor or lawyer does not by any means guarantee that the same level of competence has been maintained. The recognised professions contain many people who, as a result of drink, senility, boredom or exhaustion, are quite unfit to practise, but who are permitted, under the shield of their all-important piece of paper, to bluff their way through the remainder of their working life. For such people, the use of jargon is exceedingly important. The strong people have no need of it, but it is a godsend to the weak.

In the following chapters we have attempted to reflect and to some extent systematise the confusion over what is and what is not a profession by creating the categories of 'near-profession' and 'would-be profession'. Teaching and museum work are near-professions, insurance and public relations are would-be professions. Expressions such as 'the profession of letters' or 'the profession of arms' we have accepted as pleasant and possibly flattering fictions. We have given the military and the politicians a chapter to themselves, because their activities and their language are so closely linked, and we have thought it useful and seemly to reserve another special section for literature and the arts, whose jargon is of a peculiar kind.

It is a curious fact that 'jargon' was first used, in the late fourteenth century, in the sense of the twittering of birds. From this it passed on naturally to mean talk one does not understand, or gibberish, and so to any form of speech or writing filled with unfamiliar terms or peculiar to a particular group of persons. It is worth pointing out, however, that there are, even in England, several English languages and that they differ from one another to such a significant extent that an outsider can make serious errors of interpretation. There is no genuinely common language, no universal means of verbal communication in Britain. Even the commonest words have come to mean, not what the dictionary says they should, but what the user wants them to. The notice in the baker's shop, 'No bread left, only wholemeal', or the waitress's 'Will you have two veg. or baked and tomatoes with your chop?' and the description of the Health Visitor as 'the tart from the clinic' are normal expressions to the members of one social group, idiocies or the twittering of birds to those of another.

It must, in fact, be a very considerable time since the English people have possessed a common language, if indeed we have ever done so since our ancestors left their Frisian islands and Scandinavian coasts. The Golden Age is certainly a long way away. There are, nevertheless, two important differences between the position now and a century ago, differences which have considerable linguistic implications. The first is that the people who work with their hands have become socially, politically and economically much more powerful, and the second is that changes in the technology of communication have made it far easier for one cultural sub-group to hear the members of another group talking. They may not necessarily like or understand what they hear, but it is placed before them for their examination. Speech communities are no longer as self-contained as they were – a fact which does not always make for increased tolerance. The more one is made aware of other people's strange ways of talking and writing, the more one may feel inclined to dismiss them as jargon.

One can put this another way by saying that the political upheavals of the past century, and the past fifty years especially, have made it easier for the working classes to sustain their special forms of jargon and more difficult for the professional classes to preserve theirs, the implication always being nowadays that whatever the common man cannot understand is socially undesirable, undemocratic. There is no longer the same tremendous gulf between the environment, the habits, the prestige and the morale of what used to be called, with good reason, the upper or middle classes on the one hand and the lower or working classes on the other. In a celebrated judgment, Lord Justice Denning ruled in the Court of Appeal[16] that the expression 'working class' must now be considered meaningless and obsolete. 'Fifty years ago,' he said, 'the phrase was well understood to mean people who worked largely by their hands, whether on the land, or on the railways, or in the mines, and who in those days earned wages which on the whole were much less than the rest of the community: but nowadays the phrase is quite inapplicable, because people, whether they work on the land, in offices, in factories, or indeed in the professions, earn very often the same amount, and craftsmen often earn as much or more than professional people.'[17]

What you earn, relative to other people, influences the way in which you think about the habits and opinions of those other people. Money is not, of course, the only factor to be considered – the relative cleanness, security and working hours of different occupations still mean quite a lot. So does the political power of the group or class to which you belong. But if you habitually earn as much as another man, the likelihood is that you will reckon yourself to be as good as he is. Your tastes, your ways of spending your leisure and, in the broad sense, of expressing yourself are the equal of his. You will adopt only those once socially superior habits, such as motor cars and refrigerators and foreign holidays, which made you feel good. Socially superior language may not make you feel good at all and you may well see no reason for adopting it. This may well mean that the 'several English languages' have been moving towards a point where their prestige is more nearly equal than it was one or two generations ago.

This argument should not be carried too far. What we call 'standard English' is still more highly thought of than any other variety. It is taught in schools, spoken by the majority of influential people and listened to on television and radio. Most people respect it as 'the best English,' even though they may choose not to adopt it for their own personal use. The 'several English languages' which we can identify today are, to a considerable extent, the results of bringing standard English into a number of different cultural situations. There is nothing ungrammatical about 'No bread left, only wholemeal' and, in their form at least, all the words belong to the standard language. But the meaning which the words carry in this context would need careful explanation to a foreigner. It reveals values which are confidently and sometimes aggressively held by one social group and scorned or misunderstood by others.

It is easy to think of similar examples. The impersonal pronoun 'one', for instance – What was one to do? One couldn't imagine such a thing – is never used at all by at least three-quarters of the English people. There are few simpler or more useful words in the language, yet it has become a recognised class-badge, with considerable potential as an irritant. To the majority of our fellow-citizens it sounds affected, standoffish, inhuman, or even downright rude, a symbol of an alien and unpleasant culture.

Such reactions are usually entirely subconscious and emotional, the product of outraged group feelings. It is normal to use language, abnormal to comment on it. In practice, even people of low intelligence and poor education acquire considerable powers of linguistic discrimination. By living year in, year out within a particular speech community, one develops a subtle feeling for that group's usages and taboos. Few people find it pleasant to be misunderstood or ostracised and it is satisfying to discover the right words to impress or influence another person. Between two members of the same social or speech group communication is usually perfectly adequate, no matter how 'badly' either or both of them may appear to speak. Serious instances of irritation or lack of comprehension usually occur only when people are attempting to talk across group frontiers. For a considerable number of people, 'No bread, only wholemeal' is a precise statement.

For the most part, we speak and write only as well as we need in order to persuade ourselves that we are being comprehended and approved. If the people with whom A regularly associates at work or in his leisure hours are satisfied with single-group standards of communication, it is unlikely that A's own command of language will go much beyond what membership of his group demands. If communication between two groups is confined to giving and taking simple orders, there is no real need for one group to be able to handle the language of the other. Domestic servants, tradesmen, criminals, social reformers and certain types of intermediary, such as salesmen, teachers and non-commissioned officers must be to some extent familiar with the English of several groups. The headmaster needs to cultivate the goodwill of his caretaker and to be sensitive to his language, because caretakers of any merit are in shorter supply than headmasters. The retired general must meet the local plumber considerably more than half-way, because retired generals are plentiful and plumbers are scarce.

Jargon, whether used by professional people or by any other sections of the community, implies a closely-knit, indentifiable occupational or social group, sometimes both. It is a way of improving the cohesion and camaraderie of the group and a defence against those who belong to other groups. It is also quicker and easier to use ready-made phrases, however well-worn or meaningless they may be, rather than to go to the trouble of thinking up precisely the right words for oneself.

The politician, like the businessman, may find that success is more probable if one rounds off the sharp edges of truth, or in some cases chooses the kind of language which obscures it altogether. He may, from the purest of motives, believe that it is kind and in the national interest to do what he can to prevent people from becoming miserable. He may feel obliged to trick them into acting in what he believes to be their best interests. He may believe that a little vagueness or a little jargon are no bad thing on occasion, to keep the people quiet and happy, while the experts get on with the skilled business of running the country or making and selling motor cars. It is not difficult to discover the public man who sincerely believes that mildly and sometimes more than mildly unscrupulous propaganda is genuinely helpful to society.

Perhaps there is nothing intrinsically immoral in such an attitude. Doctors, lawyers and priests have used jargon as extensively and as deliberately as politicians are likely to want to, and they can fairly point to the useful, socially-responsible work which has been done behind the smoke-screens. The danger is that deception will run away with itself. The habitual use of language which is blown-up or meaningless, but which has high emotional value, ultimately rots the minds of the people who speak or write it. It leads to a failure to understand plain English or, even worse, to a failure to want to understand it. Plain English can, of course, be dynamite. History is littered with the remains of men who failed to understand the perils of calling a spade a spade.

With any example of jargon or propaganda, one has first to ask, 'For whom is this intended? Is it strictly in-stuff, masonic expressions for initiates only, or is it directed at a wider audience? Is the author using it deliberately as a means of sorting out the sheep from the goats? Was he trying to say to the world, in effect, "Admire me. I am a great expert, a superior being, who can handle words which mean nothing to the rank and file of my fellow-citizens." Or has he reached the point at which the use of such language is automatic, so that the choice of this word rather than that is no longer within his control?'

In the chapters which follow, the problem of intention will be frequently explored in connexion with particular professions. At this stage it may be helpful to discuss the matter in a more general way, with examples selected across the occupational range. This will, perhaps, help to make it clear that one is investigating the climate of our times, not attacking particular professions for their corruption or lack of social responsibility.

Herbert Marcuse has noted a remarkable paradox in the way in which words are used now, in the second half of the twentieth century. On the one hand there is a liveliness in developing new words and phrases, which recalls the first Elizabethan age, and on the other the deadening, flattening effect of the institutions of political, bureaucratic and industrial power, which accustoms the whole population to accept formulae as a normal form of expression. Private speech, one could say, is vigorous and prospering, public speech is dead before it is born.

> Slang and colloquial speech [writes Marcuse] have rarely been so creative. It is as if the common man (or his anonymous spokesman) would in his speech assert his humanity against the powers that be, as if the rejection and revolt, subdued in the political sphere, would burst out in the vocabulary that calls things by their names: 'head-shrinker' and 'egghead', 'boob tube', 'think tank', 'beat it' and 'dig it', and 'gone, man, gone'.[18]

However, he goes on,

> The defense laboratories and the executive offices, the governments and the machines, the time-keepers and managers, the efficiency experts and the political beauty parlors (which provide the leaders with the appropriate make-up) speak a different language and, for the time being, they seem to have the last word. It is the word that orders and organises, that induces people to do, to buy and to accept. It is transmitted in a style which is a veritable linguistic creation; a syntax in which the structure of the sentence is abridged and condensed in such a way that no tension, no 'space' is left between the parts of the sentence. This linguistic form militates against a development of meaning.[19]

This offers us the picture of a tug-of-war, with the life-team pulling in one direction and the death-team in the other, and the death-team, in Marcuse's view, showing strong signs of winning. The most unfortunate aspect of the problem is that the members of the winning side, assuming Marcuse to be correct in his analysis, hold much of the power and therefore much of the money in today's society. Their example is consequently highly infectious. If jargon is seen to be an accompaniment and possibly a corollary of power, ambitious people in other occupations are all too likely to see jargon as a necessary item in their career-kit. Certain kinds of people are particularly at risk. One can identify them as:

1. Those who are insecure and who feel they must do everything possible to make society feel that it needs their services.
2. Those who are ashamed of what they do and are driven to find suitable language with which to gild their activities.
3. Those who need big words, as they need big cars, to give them an extra ration of size.
4. Those who have nothing really to sell, and who need jargon in order to hoodwink the customers.

For one or more of these reasons, the most notorious jargon-producers at the present time are politicians and political propagandists, East and West; those engaged in the social sciences, particularly in psychology;

spokesmen for the armed forces; people writing about or publicising hotels, restaurants and the entertainment industry; economists and management experts; writers on education; bureaucrats; and critics of literature and the arts. Doctors and lawyers, by comparison with these major offenders, are much less given to jargon nowadays, a fact which is likely to surprise anyone who has not looked at a selection of medical literature for some time, if at all. Engineers, architects and designers usually speak and write in a straightforward manner, except when they are infected by the management or planning virus. The clergy and other people who are called upon to express themselves on religious subjects must reckon to devote most of their energy to explaining what they mean by a number of key theological terms. Of all the professions, they are forced to wrestle hardest and most continuously with the problem of explaining their technical vocabulary, of making jargon intelligible.

In her classic study of America's war in Vietnam, Mary McCarthy presents a terrifying picture of an enormous national effort which was fuelled on jargon. We are shown the aide who 'steps forward to state "We sterilize the area prior to the insertion of the R.D. teams", whose task, says the colonel, is to find out "the aspiration of the people".'[20] A glossary is required to interpret such a passage. 'Sterilising' an area means burning down all human habitations, together with much of the vegetation, and removing the people to concentration camps, where they can be instructed in the virtues of the American free-enterprise system and in the evils of Communism. 'R.D. teams' are Rural Development teams, who put the people back into villages newly built to receive them and help them to create another, approved and better kind of life for themselves. 'The aspiration of the people' is never investigated too deeply, in case it should turn out to mean simply to be allowed to live in peace, instead of being passionately anxious to defeat the Communist forces from the North.

> If [says Mary McCarthy] you ask a junior officer what he thinks our war aims are in Vietnam, he usually replies without hesitation: 'To punish aggression'. It is unkind to try to draw him into a discussion of what constitutes aggression and what is defense (the Bay of Pigs, Santo Domingo, Goa?) for he really has no further ideas on the subject. He has been indoctrinated, just as much as the North P.O.W., who tells the interrogation team he is fighting to 'liberate the native soil from the American aggressors' – maybe more. Only, the young American does not know it; he probably imagines that he is *thinking* when he produces that formula.[21]

The almost unbelievable Professor Wesley Fishel, of Michigan State University, was established in Vietnam as a political-philosophical adviser to the American authorities. He proved himself to be one of the world's leading masters of jargon. His lasting contribution was the introduction of the word 'semantics' into official discourse about Vietnam. 'We do ourselves and our Asian neighbours harm when we insist on stretching or shrinking them into our particular semantic bed,' he wrote in *The New Leader,* arguing for 'a new political vocabulary' in an article wonderfully entitled (Professor Fishel claims by the editors) 'Vietnam's Democratic One-Man Rule' – the Procrustean subject was Diem. A democratic 'dictator', or a 'democratic' dictator? Words failed Professor Fishel. Diem has gone, but embarrassments of the kind he created have not. Almost daily in the press briefing, whenever a newsman raises his hand to ask for clarification of some mealy-mouthed statement: 'I am not going to debate semantics with you,' the spokesman replies. 'Next?'[22]

Professor Fishel was clearly a man who had brought the stifling of awkward questions to a fine academic art. To say 'I am not going to debate semantics with you' is much more final and professional-sounding than 'I am not going to argue with you', which is all the sentence means. But it is the extreme and most unscrupulous form of jargon, amounting to a deliberate confidence trick. It recalls the achievements of another master of verbal conjuring, the late Dr Josef Goebbels, who earned his exalted position in the Nazi hierarchy by his skill in making his listeners and readers believe nonsense. His famous peroration, at a mass meeting of Westphalian farmers in the 1930s, has the classic quality which would have won the admiration of Professor Fishel. Pausing for tumultous applause after each statement, he said, or rather shouted: 'We don't want higher bread prices. We don't want lower bread prices. We don't want the same bread prices. We want National Socialist bread prices.' Thirty years later, when the cover-up business had become more sophisticated and the terminology had been brought up-to-date, Dr Goebbels might well have silenced a difficult member of his audience by saying 'I am not going to debate semantics with you.'

Most of the examples discussed in the present book are not as sinister as Professor Fishel's semantics and Dr Goebbels' bread prices. They are the product of confused minds, super-conventional minds, pompous minds, ambitious minds, half-educated minds and woolly minds, but not, on the whole, of criminal or dangerously warped minds.

There are the social scientists, protecting their status with such word-shields as 'Teachers with an activist orientation risk administrative sanction';[23] 'With language as a cultural product embodying the typifications sedimented in the history of the society';[24] 'The largely humanist-oriented intellectual dissenter is being rapidly displaced by the generalist-integrators, who become in effect house idealogues for those in power';[25] and 'This problem is avoided by sufficient interviewer orientation before the actual interviews'.[26]

A musicologist will tell us that 'We thus had the direct experience of a *lasting* meta-personal inspiration, expanses of calm, dimensional plurality, freedom, spaciousness, and of a medial self-renunciation transcending all our previous experiences',[27] and a psychologist will ask us to 'recall again that we conceive of the disbelief system as a similarity continuum. Recall also the parallel representation of a "pantheon" of negative authorities arranged in terms of similarity to one's positive authority. We will now add here the further suggestion that corresponding to these disbelief and negative authority continua is also a disbeliever continuum. Adherents to various disbelief subsystems may also be seen by the person in terms of a continuum of similarity to adherents of his own belief system. In other words, the world of people is organised not merely in terms of ingroup and outgroups, but in terms of ingroup and a continuum of outgroups.'[28]

Educational research and theory will prove to be a rich reef for the jargon prospector. We shall find such nuggets as 'His current research interests focus on attitudinal changes in college students and group counselling with college underachievers';[29] 'Students whose primary orientation to college is vocational';[30] and 'In order to identify the underlying dimensions of teacher behavior, these variables were factor-analysed, using the principal factors method. Ten factors were extracted, accounting for 73 per cent of the variance. These were rotated to orthogand simple structure by the varimax method.'[31]

Much useful material can be turned up in the course of reading the literature and advertisements of business management, typical examples being: 'The key task will be to lead the continued development of the manufacturing operations whilst effectively accommodating the current demands of a volatile market';[32] 'Supported by a strong multi-discipline team, your principal objective will be to maximise the contribution to the operation, within a work environment which is constructive and positive';[33] 'Members of our account management groups are given early accountability for providing a comprehensive recruitment service to a number of clients with diverse activities';[34] and, delightfully, 'You must be an enthusiastic self-starter, preferably with a motor manufacturer'.[35]

Politics and the official bureaucracies will be well to the front, with such dignified phrases as 'word processing unit', the current Canadian government jargon for a typing-pool, and such Left-wing in-language as 'convince teachers that their true interests lie with the laboring proletariat',[36] and 'trailing behind the Trotskyite anti-Communist gangs of thugs'.[37] Important public men will display their talent for saying nothing impressively with statements of the type of 'Obviously we all appreciate the frankest possible speaking at the United Nations and elsewhere, but it is not necessarily my view that that kind of speaking is good for either the Western Alliance or the United Nations'.[38]

The advertisers have a great deal to contribute. We shall enjoy learning that 'the Westhofener Steingrube is rich and more expansive with good finishing grip';[39] that 'the 1970 is a profound, long wine',[40] and that 'Yves St. Laurent's Triangles give even more design impact to your bed'.[41] It will be reassuring to know that a leading American is in a position to sell us clothes which will be 'a sum of many compatible parts to communicate your personal fashion statement'.[42]

To escape from such demanding prose, we may well find it a comfort and a relaxation to spend a few minutes each day reading what judges have said and written in recent years. What is called their jargon is, ironically, often nothing else but English used with extreme precision. In an age in which poor, muddled, pompous language is almost normal, to express oneself clearly and in a disciplined manner is to render oneself vulnerable to the charge of speaking jargon. Black has become white, and war is now peace.

'We are not the slaves of words but their masters,' said the Master of the Rolls, Lord Denning, in 1967. 'We sit here to give them their natural and ordinary meaning in the context in which we find them'.[43] Judges, unlike advertisers and certain other categories of people, serve the community by trying to use words in such a way that no misunderstanding is possible. It is a formidable task, demanding an intellect of the highest quality. To listen to legal decision delivered by a judge on his best form is, for those who are connoisseurs of language, a very great pleasure. The simplest and most everyday words can be surrounded with perils and pitfalls, which it is a judge's duty to remove. Consider, for example, the term 'litter'. This, under Section 1 of the Litter Act of 1958, can consist of 'anything whatsoever' if it is 'thrown down, dropped or otherwise deposited in, into or from any place in the open air to which the public are entitled or permitted to have access without payment, and left there, unless authorised by law or done with the consent of the owner, etc. of the place'.[44]

To the layman, such a definition might appear almost ludicrously careful and foolproof. But, in practice, the word 'deposited' was found to be far from precise and a source of considerable disagreement, until the Lord Chief Justice applied his skill and experience to the matter.

> It is quite clear [he said] that not only the depositing but also the leaving is necessary, because it was not intended that an offence should be committed if somebody deposited litter and immediately cleared it up. Accordingly, although the act constituting the offence consists of throwing down, dropping or otherwise depositing, it is only an offence if it is not removed. The offence is not committed unless both of these things, the depositing and the leaving, occur. Depositing is an act fixed in point of time and not a continuing matter, and accordingly I am quite satisfied that this cannot be treated as a continuing offence.[45]

In 1942 the Chief Justice of the United States, Mr Justice Frankfurter, received a letter from a boy of twelve who announced his ambition to be a lawyer one day and asked for advice on how to proceed in the meantime. The Chief Justice wrote back encouragingly, telling the boy to forget about the law for several years and to concentrate on improving his mind and his appreciation of language by reading good literature, looking at good pictures and generally learning to be a cultured, civilised person. Only then, he said, would the young man be prepared to begin his legal studies with any prospect of real success. 'No one,' he wrote, 'can be a truly competent lawyer unless he is a cultivated man. The best way to prepare for the law is to come to the study of the law as a well-read person. Thus alone can one acquire the capacity to use the English language on paper and in speech and with the habits of clear thinking which only a truly liberal education can give.'[46] The advice is not only applicable to would-be lawyers. Jargon is the product of an insensitive, uneducated mind. A properly educated person cannot bring himself to use it, and the sad truth is that a very large number of the highly educated people who control our lives today and to whom society gives the greatest prestige and reward have received a most inadequate and unbalanced education. Among other failings, they have never acquired a mastery of their mother-tongue.

For both professional and philosophical reasons, scientists and near-scientists have come to believe that the best kind of language is one which betrays no sign of the author's personality or even existence and which is hard, clear and unambiguous, a language which is tidy and exact, with no synonyms and with all possibilities of misunderstanding removed. Confined to the scientific and technical fields, and possibly the legal field, too, such thinking may be entirely reasonable.

There is, however, a danger in the situation. It is that people may come to believe that all human activities can be satisfactorily analysed and described in this same 'hard, clear and unambiguous language' and that what cannot be proved by methods of science cannot be true. If routine tests can be devised for chemicals, then one must be found for hunger or the intelligence of children. The untested part is not allowed to be built into the engine and the untested child cannot enter the school. The human personality, according to some modern investigators, can be examined in substantially the same way as the physical structure of a hydrocarbon. 'The essence of high F is a placid, unemotional, realistic cheerfulness, with talkativeness, geniality, enthusiasm and a witty originality. All factorizations stress cheerful joyousness, gregariousness, friendly assertiveness and talkativeness, adaptability, quick resourcefulness, humour that tends to wit, and (less definite), sympathy, curiosity and trustfulness'.[47]

The nineteenth century was not exposed to this appalling temptation, partly because scientists and technicians were relatively few and unimportant and partly for a reason which has been excellently stated by Professor Lionel Trilling: 'In the nineteenth century, in this country as in Europe, literature underlay every activity of mind. The scientist, the philosopher, the historian, the theologian, the economist, the social theorist, and even the politician were required to command literary abilities which would now be thought irrelevant to their respective callings.'[48]

Half-way through the twentieth century there can be no doubt at all that literature does not 'underlie every activity of mind'. The various professions do not move within the same community of culture. There is, broadly speaking, a scientific culture and there is a culture based on letters. The last three-quarters of a century has tried hard, but on the whole without success, to achieve some kind of synthesis between them. Nowadays many observers believe that such a synthesis is impossible, that either science or humanism must conquer the other. And science seems determined to win. The technological revolution of the twentieth century shows signs of handling the humanities much more roughly than the Industrial Revolution of the nineteenth did. It has been stressing the intellect to a degree which is both dangerous and absurd.[49]

In our world of violent emotions and dogmas there is – and it is as well to admit it – something attractive about the kind of language which makes real understanding more likely. There is a genuine feeling of pride in being able to handle a specialised vocabulary properly. We should be careful of attacking any kind of mental discipline. If the generous but correct use of technical terms tones up a man's mind, there is clearly much to be said for it. It is interesting to find technical writing defended in much the same terms that were frequently heard used in praise of a classical education: 'For though technical terms form only a small fraction of the words used in any piece of writing, the precision with which they have to be employed has, I think, had a good effect on the thinking and writing of engineers. When he is forced to exercise extreme care with some of his most important words an author will acquire the habit of exercising similar care with others.'[50]

This may be so, but it seems equally likely that logic will kill subtlety, that language will lose its overtones and therefore its possibilities. It was George Orwell's nightmare when he envisaged Newspeak, the English in which 'every concept that can ever be needed will be expressed by exactly *one* word, with its meaning rigidly defined and all its subsidiary meanings rubbed out and forgotten'.[51]

The scientific-technological revolution could quite well lead to this result. It has produced large numbers of people who rate the logical, no-synonym language highly, including many routine research workers who are little more than post-graduate slaves, whether they are employed in

University laboratories or by industrial firms. It could develop a mechanised way of spending leisure which would make individual effort seem old-fashioned. Anyone who, like Orwell, sits down to see how far the process has gone already may come to frightening conclusions.

But it is not inevitable that the logical conclusion will be reached. Since the dropping of the first atomic bomb, scientists have become aware of the dangers of rational, scientific man. They have come to realise that the mind of the complete man needs more than science to feed it. If a person cannot see the virtues of scientific language, he is out of tune with his age. If, on the other hand, he is unable to appreciate the poet's language, he is cut off from much of his national heritage. He must acknowledge that both kinds of language are important to him.

The only way of keeping jargon under control is to make sure that people of the highest intelligence receive a broadly-based education, the most important part of which is the development of a pride in handling words really well. If we could achieve this, we could forget about jargon. It would simply wither away, as the members of our old and new professional groups got the linguistic chip off their shoulders.

1 The Learned Professions

The 'learned professions' are traditionally reckoned to be the Church, Medicine and the Law, and there seems to be no reason to add to the list. These were normal careers for university graduates throughout the Middle Ages and until the Industrial Revolution made it possible for a person who had attended a university to think of other ways of making a respectable living. They were called the 'learned professions' because entry to them was restricted to men who had followed a course in the humanities and were accepted as scholars. How many of today's clergy, lawyers and doctors would consider themselves scholars is an open question, but no great harm is done by giving them the benefit of the doubt. What they have always had in common, however, has been considerable social prestige, although that of the clergy is rather less now than it was a century ago, and the requirement, as an inevitable part of their position and duty, to function as linguistic middle men, people who allowed a certain amount of professional jargon to filter through to the general public. Most of them have earned a living, often a very handsome living, by interpreting scholarly knowledge to their fellow citizens and by applying it to the task of holding society together and helping it to function.

This has been especially true of the clergy. Over the centuries they have brought educated speech into places where very little of it would otherwise have been heard, they have listened to humble people talking about their difficulties and their fears, they have learnt to speak simply to simple people and, Sunday after Sunday, they have given all classes of men and women an opportunity to absorb the traditional rhythms of the Bible and the liturgy. This is not, of course, to say that all clergy have functioned equally successfully in this way – some, in all periods, have been idle, some have been pure scholars, and the personal culture of others has left a good deal to be desired[1] – or that all parts of the country have benefited equally. Large numbers of people in the major industrial areas, for instance, remained untouched by any religious influence throughout the nineteenth century, no matter how God-fearing Victorian England may have considered itself. But the assured presence within a compact area of one reasonably well-educated man, with a duty to use his education for the common good, and of a building in which people of a wide range of occupations and social levels could assemble on Sundays must have introduced a great many people to English better than their own.

English pulpit styles have been nearly as varied as English clergymen. We have had the lively manner of Bishop Hall:

> Here was Adam, delving with a jaw-bone, and harrowing with sticks tied uncouthly together, and paring his nails with his teeth: there was Eve, making a comb of her fingers, and tying her raw-skinned breeches together with rinds of trees; or pinning them up with thorns.[2]

We have had Archbishop Tillotson's careful philosophising in colloquial vocabulary and uncolloquial rhythms:

> Now the best in the world for a man to seem to be any thing, is really to be what he would seem to be. Besides, that it is many times as troublesome to make good the pretence of a good quality as to have it; and if a man have it not, it is ten to one, but he is discovered to want it, and then all his pains and labour to seem to have it is lost. There is something unnatural in Painting, which a skilful Eye will easily discern from Native Beauty and Complexion.[3]

We have had the metaphysical sermons of John Donne:

> We die every day, and we die all the day long; and because we are not absolutely dead, we call that an eternity, an eternity of dying: And is there comfort in that state? Why, that is the state of hell itself, Eternal dying, and not dead.[4]

And, it is hardly necessary to add, we have had tens of thousands of sermons at all periods when the skill and erudition of the preacher has fallen behind that of Hall and Tillotson and Donne. From the pastoral and theological point of view that may be a bad thing, but from a linguistic point of view all that matters is that the parson shall handle words better than the average member of his congregation. And surely there can have been few instances when this has not been the case?

Sometimes, of course, the sermon may have been so far above the congregation's head as to resemble pure sound. Swift noted early in the eighteenth century that the clergy were overgiven to using words like ominiscience, omnipresence, ubiquity and beatific, which meant nothing to the ordinary churchgoer.[5] But, as Bishop Smith remarked in a sermon preached in 1668, [6] those who were 'the fondest of high-flown metaphors and allegories, attended and set off with scraps of Greek and Latin' were ignorant and illiterate country people, who were equally pleased by the wonderful strings of exotic names to be found in the books of the Old Testament. These simple people found a great deal of enjoyment and education in their church services. The Bible and the Prayer Book always, and the sermon, one hopes, fairly frequently, showed them what could be done with English by men who were skilled in speaking and writing it. There are those who believe that the influence of the Authorised Version has been pernicious. Somerset Maugham held this view very strongly. 'Blunt Englishmen,' he says, 'twisted their tongues to speak like Hebrew Prophets'.[7] The opinion more commonly found is that of George Saintsbury, who was sure that the Jacobean Bible had been the means 'by which three centuries of readers and hearers have had kept before them the prowess and the powers of the English tongue'.[8]

But, however beautiful the language of the Authorised Version may be, it is over three hundred and fifty years old and commonly said by churchmen to be no longer understood by large sections of the British people. For this reason, a Joint Committee of the Churches decided, in 1946, that a new translation of the original text was essential, 'frankly contemporary in vocabulary, idiom, style and rhythm'.[9] The New English Bible is the result, produced, like the Authorised Version, by a committee of scholars.[10] Whether it is any easier to understand by people who are neither Christians nor familiar with the language of Christian theology, is something which can only be proved by practice and experiment. It is quite possible, of course, that the reason why so much of the Authorised Version seems like a foreign language to a high proportion of twentieth century Englishmen is not because its phraseology is archaic, but because it is technical.

To the person who is not a practising Christian, I doubt if:

> God is light, and in him there is no darkness at all. If we claim to be sharing in his life while we walk in the dark, our words and our lives are a lie; but if we walk in the light as he himself is in the light, then we share together a common life, and we are being cleansed from every sin by the blood of Jesus his Son.

is any more meaningful than:

> God is light, and in him is no darkness at all. If we say that we have fellowship with him, and walk in darkness, we lie, and do not tell the truth: But if we walk in the light, as he is in the light, we have fellowship one with another, and the blood of Jesus Christ his Son cleanseth us from all sin.

To anyone who is unfamiliar with Christian phraseology, both the Authorised Version and the New English Bible are likely to sound like jargon or, in extreme cases, gibberish.

There is a form of speaking and writing practised by religious people, whether members of the clergy or not, which is certainly not the language of everyday life. It is still being produced and fully deserves the label 'religious English'. Here is an example, a prayer written and published in the 1950s.

> Eternal God, who dost call all men into unity with Thy Son, Jesus Christ our Lord, we pray Thee to pour Thy spirit upon the students of all nations, that they may consecrate themselves to Thy service; that by being joined together by their common faith and obedience, they may come more perfectly to love and understand one another, that the world may know that Thou didst send Thy Son to be the Saviour and the Lord of all men; through the same Jesus Christ our Lord Who with Thee and the Holy Spirit liveth and reigneth one God world without end. Amen.[11]

To say that this prayer is made from a kit of religious parts would be, perhaps, a little unkind, but it is a form of composition that can be easily acquired. How much it means to the author one cannot say, but to anyone who lives outside the world of Christian belief and observance it must appear pure jargon.

Occasionally, one find striking evidence of the deep impression which religious language is capable of making on uneducated people. John Wesley, for instance, records the following conversation which he had with the wife of a Spitalfields weaver.

> 'When did you know your sins were forgiven?'
>
> 'Yesterday, between three and four in the afternoon, while Mr. Manners was at prayer.'
>
> 'When was you so filled with the love of God?'
>
> 'About eight in the evening. I was then taken away by the angels and carried where I saw a great lake of fire, and I saw abundance of people chained down in it, and I heard their groans. Then they took me into heaven; and I saw all the holy angels round the throne of God; and I sung with them. And I saw God. I did not see him like a man, but as a glorious brightness. I cannot tell you how it was, but it was three and one'.

It is easy enough to smile at the naive attempts of the Spitalfields woman to put her vision into the proper phrases. But the point is that she felt impelled to try, and that attendance at religious meetings had allowed her to have the appropriate words available when she needed them. Her religion had given her what was in effect a second language, in which she could express the highest thoughts and feelings of which she was capable.

To the irreligious it may seem nonsensical jargon, mere babbling, but to her it was something that helped her to pull herself out of the dreariness and pointlessness of her everyday existence.

She was, in this respect, a good deal more fortunate than many, perhaps most, people at the present time, who have no contact at all with either religion or poetry and who are consequently deprived of any language in which their minds and spirits can rise above daily routine. For the majority of people of all classes, religious practice has always been the chief and often the only means by which they have become familiar with the poetic possibilities of language. It is not, of course, the only possible means available to mankind; the poetic spirit can be kindled in a tube train or on the top of Everest. But the alternatives to religion remain well-concealed and with regular churchgoing largely a matter of the past, few people at the present time seem to have access to a language which encourages their minds and their emotions to develop very far above clichés.

Over the centuries, the clergy, of varying degrees of scholarship, have toiled to make the language of the Bible comprehensible to ordinary people. They have paraphrased it, preached whole sermons on a particular phrase, told stories to bring out its meaning, dramatised it. One may say, cynically, that they had a vested interest in doing so, but one can also believe that, however devoted and admirable their professional efforts to make the Bible seem plain and straightforward may have been they were doomed to inevitable and continuous failure. As an expert on religious language has put it, 'No attempt to make the language of the Bible conform to a precise, straightforward language – whether that language be scientific or historical – has ever succeeded. The "facts" of the Gospels in particular are never facts for which science is appropriate currency; or history is appropriate currency. The language of the Bible, and of the Gospels in particular, must be odd enough to be appropriate to the odd situations which are their subject'.[13]

But the Bible, like a Shakespeare sonnet, is not jargon, whether one understands it or not. The jargon comes from the people who attempt to tell us what the Bible means and to preach the Christian message. The parallel with the Shakespearian scholars and critics is exact, and depressing.

One does not have to search hard or far to find notable jargon-mongers in the field of religion. Dr Frank Buchman, the founder of Moral Rearmament and the greatest jargon man of them all, will do very well. Speaking to a World Assembly for the Moral Rearmament of the Nations at Mackinac Island, Michigan, in 1960, Dr Buchman proclaimed:

> 'My deep personal wish is to have every American free under the direction of God to fight for America; so to fight that America really be free, free from the tyranny of sin, under God's direction, the unseen

but ever-present Power. I wish this no less deeply for everyone in every nation.

'I don't want our sons, especially our fighting sons, to go about without an answer. It simply enslaves them. It is not good enough. It will drive them to the same philosophy that rules our opponents. We shall never create an inspired democracy that way. Men must learn to have a faith that will create the right revolution. If we can spread this revolution fast enough we can save America and the world. Unless we have this revolution there will be a revolution of chaos.

'It needs this stronger dose. Sin leaves us with such a dull heavy thud. "The blood of Jesus Christ His Son cleanseth us from all sin." That is the discovery everyone is looking for. That is the answer.'

Dr Buchman, like John Wesley, was a revivalist, not a scholar. He aimed at the heart and the nervous system, not the head, and he was well aware of the value of religious jargon as a means of sweeping an audience off its feet and of attracting the contributions and the converts in the most gratifying manner. There have certainly been medical men who have shown by their skilful technique of first stimulating fear and then showing how it can be set at rest, that their attitude to their work is not very different from Dr Buchman's.[14] This is hardly surprising, since medicine and religion have a common ritual ancestry.

The matter of medical jargon has been briefly touched on above in the introductory chapter. An assessment of its present strength has to begin with at least a glance at its origins. Early medicine was thought of as a 'mystery', just as some of the early religious sects were 'mysteries'. The body of knowledge which medical practitioners had accumulated was carefully safeguarded, in order that it should not be available to the community as a whole. It was at least semi-secret and the doctor's power required that it should remain so. This caused the first great distinction between a doctor who had the key to the mysteries, and his patients, who did not. A further distinction came later, when it became necessary for qualified doctors and surgeons to protect themselves against unqualified practitioners. This became a matter of importance during the Renaissance, when the frontiers of knowledge were being rapidly extended and when medicine embraced, in addition to technical competence, various branches of theology, astrology, alchemy and demonology. In 1565 Dr John Hall, who considered the reputation of his profession to be at stake, found the position serious enough to warrant the publication of an *Historical Expostulation against the Beastly Abusers both of Chirurgerie and Physike in our Tyme with Goodlye Doctrine and Instruction necessarye to be marked and followed of all true Chirurgiens.* The seventeenth century saw the rise of empiricism, first as a rival and then as a partner to medical theory, and, to some extent, the idea and the possibility of specialisation emerged at this time.

Doctors, in other words, came to exclude the lay public to protect both themselves and their profession. It was almost inevitable that they should have done so, since the gulf between their education and that of the common man was so wide. And, with certain reservations, this is still true. One is faced therefore with a paradox, that the members of the general public are inevitably in close connection with the medical profession – they are its raw material – and yet they are rigidly excluded from it. This is both the cause and the result of communication difficulties, which are of two kinds:

1. The practical difficulties which arise because of the patient's inability to describe his symptoms accurately and the doctor's inability to satisfy his patient's desire to know about his condition. The two do not speak the same language.
2. The effect of popularisation on medical language, causing it to be less precise than doctors know it should be.

The problem is not, however, confined to communication between doctors and their patients. There are difficulties of communication too, between doctors themselves. Some of these are historical and some linguistic in origin. The new medical knowledge which was acquired during the Renaissance was too extensive to fit the old terms which had been used by Hippocrates and Galen, and much of it contradicted the premises on which these terms had originally been based. But, since they were hallowed by authority and use, they continued to be employed, although they were clearly inadequate and often misleading. 'Lymph', 'nerve' and 'hysteria' are cases in point. This led to a confusion which has never been entirely resolved.

The literary and figurative use of medical terms has also bedevilled communication. The figurative uses tend to establish their own field of meaning, which is often quite unconnected with the original scientific meaning. 'Heart-strings', for instance, was once a medical term, but later became primarily an image with musical implications.

There are other problems involving medical language. The incidental, and unintended, communication between a doctor and his patients which can occur in the course of a teaching round, when the doctor is primarily concerned with communicating with his students, can cause considerable misunderstanding and fear. Advertisers know and exploit the interest which ordinary people have in medical matters and not infrequently mislead the public quite deliberately in this way.

The popularisation, by both doctors and their patients, of some medical words which were at first non-medical has been due to the public's desire to find euphemisms for terms which they know well enough to find frightening. This tendency seems to be decreasing slightly at the present time.

It is perhaps significant that there were several euphemisms for pulmonary tuberculosis, the great scourge of nineteenth-century England, whereas at present there is no widely accepted euphemism for cancer.

The problem of having an increasing amount of knowledge and too few terms to communicate that knowledge is unsolved. The word 'cell', for instance, is used differently by botanists and zoologists. But since a term must usually be applied to a disease, or to some new factor, long before all the relevant facts about it have been discovered, the difficulty is to some extent unavoidable. Terms are continuously being refined and made more precise, but one has to use them today, not wait for tomorrow. If this hazard is understood, it need not affect the ability of most medical terms to communicate with reasonable adequacy within the present limits of knowledge.

The successful populariser of medicine, as of any other body of scientific knowledge, is always aware of the compromise he is making. Sometimes, but not often, his conscience or his fear of professional criticism compels him to issue a warning to the reader. The psychologist, H. J. Eysenck, speaks for many others when he says:

> There is one great difficulty in presenting an account of psychological experiments and conclusions in popular terms, a difficulty equally great with that which besets the physicist trying to give a clear picture of what he is doing. The results of the physicist are expressed in mathematical terms, and even with the greatest ingenuity it is often impossible to translate them into ordinary language. Similarly, the results of the psychologist are so closely tied up with mathematics and statistics that an adequate understanding is impossible without at least a smattering of knowledge in these fields.[15]
>
> I have tried to leave out complex and difficult material as far as possible in this book, and have eschewed almost completely the mention of mathematics or statistics. This inevitably means that many statements are much less precise than they would otherwise have been, and the reader who feels critical of any particular statement, before voicing his criticism should remember the handicap under which the writer has been labouring.[16]

When Professor Eysenck is not popularising, when he is writing, so to speak, with his professional brakes off, he is likely to adopt quite a different style of communication, of which the following would be a fair example.

> In essence, our problem is this. We wish to find a set of weights in order to derive from our four tests a composite score for each *S* such that the square of the correlation ratio (R^2) between that composite variate and

the three groups is at a maximum. Hence, if we take $R^2 = \grave{u}Bu/\grave{u}Gu$, following Lubin (1950), we arrive at the equation $(G^{-1} B - R^2 1)u = 0$. (In this expression G and B have already been defined, u is the column vector of weights and $\grave{u}$ is its transpore. 1 is the unit diagonal matrix.) The values of R^2 which satisfy this equation are the latent roots of the non-symmetric matrix $G^{-1}B$, each root having a corresponding latent vector u.[17]

A perusal of recent medical literature, published in both Britain and America, suggests that very few doctors, no matter what their speciality, achieve the same peak of technical language as one finds in the passage just quoted. Much of what they write for consumption by other doctors is, in fact, comprehensible by the non-medical educated person who is willing to make the effort, possibly with a little help from the dictionary from time to time. The title may be formidably technical, but the article or the book itself can present the intelligent layman with few difficulties and even, indeed, verge on the readable.

One or two examples will make the point and perhaps help to convince the reader that, whatever may be true of the psychologists, those who write about human physical ailments and their treatment do not appear to need to use great quantities of jargon in order to increase their confidence in themselves.

Consider for instance the following extracts for a paper on the habit of glue-sniffing, contributed to *The Practitioner*, a British periodical written and edited by doctors for doctors.

> Despite reports in the medical literature (mainly North American) of deliberate solvent inhalation by young people, little has so far appeared in British journals and it would seem that doctors are reluctant to admit the existence of the problem in Britain. In the past few years, however, an increasing number of children in Lanarkshire, Glasgow, Renfrewshire and Ayrshire (and probably elsewhere if we did but know it) have adopted glue-sniffing as the latest craze. The chance of being called upon to treat a patient under the influence of glue, or of glue and alcohol combined, has become more likely, and it seems only reasonable to alert medical practitioners to the fact that solvent sniffing has not only reared its ugly head in a number of communities but is already taking its toll of human life. There is a wide range of solvent substances available and their easy accessibility renders the practice well-nigh impossible to control.
>
> The sniffer may be brought to the attention of a medical practitioner in one of three main ways. First, he or she may be referred by the police because of some factor associated with the glue-sniffing, such as theft or antisocial acts of disorderly conduct. Secondly, the referral

may come from the social work department, the staff of which may have been notified by the school authorities when a child is found to have been sniffing glue at school. Thirdly, the sniffer may be admitted to hospital as a result of the episode and thus, eventually, becomes the responsibility of his or her family doctor.[18]

The author then moves on, perfectly properly, to an account, in technical language, of the medical details.

Of twelve glue-sniffers studied in 1962 at the National Clearinghouse for Poison Control Centers, Salt Lake City, eight had abnormal urinary findings with protoinuria or increased numbers of white cells, or both. All had normal blood counts. In the series of studies of glue-sniffers undertaken by Press and Done (1967), one-third were found to have microscopic pyuria and this was also found by Sokol and Robinson (1963). Microscopic haematuria was also noted in a proportion of the cases. In 1965 Powars investigated six patients who had been sniffing glue, five of whom had homozygous sickle-cell disease. They developed erythrocytic aplastic crises, secondary to glue-sniffing. Recovery was rapid and complete in five after the offending agent was discontinued. The sixth patient, previously normal, died from aplastic anaemia. A case of generalized exfoliative dermatitis following exposure to paint-thinner (Samitz, 1961) caused diagnostic problems, and Hodgkin's disease and drug sensitization (?penicillin) were considered.[19]

There is nothing here that could be called jargon, nothing which could have been put more simply. The proportion of technical to 'ordinary' language will, of course, vary with the subject and from one part of an article to another, according to whether the author is describing or dis-discussing. Pure description will tend to have a high concentration of technicalities, as this passage from the *American Journal of Surgery* shows:

II. *In Vivo Suture Dissolution Studies*
Materials and Methods
Next, the rate of dissolution of these sutures was compared in the stomach, duodenum, jejunum, and colon of seven dogs. A laparotomy was performed using sodium pentobarbital anesthesia and within each organ, strands of 3–0 plain catgut, Dexon and Vicryl were anchored to the wall 3 cm. apart and allowed to lie free in the lumen. The suture was placed through the entire thickness of the wall of the viscus and tied over a Dacron bolster placed on the serosal side. A lead x-ray marker of different configuration was tied on the luminal side of each

> loop so that the identity of the suture could be ascertained postoperatively by abdominal x-rays. X-ray films were taken on the day of surgery and daily thereafter until all the markers had disappeared. Comparison of sequential films revealed the time each marker dislodged, indicating the time of absorption or disruption of the suture.[20]

This is economical and perfectly clear. It is an excellent piece of communication, written by surgeons for the benefit of surgeons.

'Mixed language', partly technical, partly general, becomes more likely when the subject is one which is much talked about by the general public. This is to some extent because, in such circumstances, doctors find it difficult to resist the pressure to meet the outside world half-way, but also because the outside world itself, helped along by television and the press, has absorbed a considerable quantity of medical terminology, more or less accurately. Coronary heart disease, blood pressure and obesity, for instance, are topics of great and urgent interest to many people in the over-fed, over-stressed Western world and such people learn, sometimes consciously, sometimes not, to speak the medical language appropriate to the disease.

Here, for instance, is part of an American article entitled 'Body fat: its relationship to Coronary Heart Disease, Blood Pressure, Lipids and other Risk Factors measured in a Large Male Population'.[21] 'Large Male Population' is not, perhaps, too happy a phrase and it could fairly be said to be jargon. The reader is likely to wonder if it means, in view of the subject, a population of large males or a large population of males. This apart, there is remarkably little jargon in the article. The summary, where the authors might possibly be expected to indulge in a little professional window-dressing, is straightforward and jargon-free:

> Obesity is variably considered to be a major contributor to hypertension and hyperlipidemia, and its treatment is recommended in the management of coronary heart disease. Total body fat was measured by tritium dilution in a large male population and its relationship to age, blood pressure, serum lipids, uric acid and the diagnoses of coronary heart disease, hypertension and glucose intolerance was examined. In addition, three commonly used weight:height indices of obesity were correlated with each of these parameters.
>
> The correlation of body fat with blood pressure, serum cholesterol and triglycerides, although statistically significant, was only of small magnitude. Mean levels of body fat were not significantly different between patients with coronary disease and control subjects, whereas serum cholesterol and, to a lesser extent, systolic blood pressure were potent risk factors for the disease. It is concluded that obesity is only a minor determinant of blood pressure and lipid level, and that its contribution to coronary heart disease is small or non-existent.[22]

The technical information in the article does exactly what is required of it:

> *Glucose intolerance* As noted in Table III, patients with glucose intolerance tended to be more obese, have higher systolic and diastolic blood pressure levels, and relatively elevated cholesterol and triglyceride levels. The mean serum uric acid level was significantly higher among older glucose intolerant patients (7.0 versus 6.5 kg/100 ml.), whereas the levels did not statistically differ in the < 40 year group (6.2 versus 6.5 mg/100 ml.).[23]

It is possible to consider 'obese' and 'obesity' jargon words, since one could equally well say 'fat' or 'overweight', but the criticism is a mild one. Equally, one could regard these words as euphemisms, at least to the lay person, although there is likely to be some disagreement as to whether it is more brutal to call someone 'fat', 'overweight' or 'obese'.

In general, one could probably say that those members of the medical profession whose concern is principally with the maladies and mishaps of the body find it fairly easy to avoid jargon or accusations of jargon, whereas those whose business is with the sick mind find themselves in much greater difficulties. The fundamental reason for this is that the greater part of their professional vocabulary has been taken over from the language of non-medical people. They have had to create the terminology they require by giving a specialised meaning to words which already exist and which have wider or different connotations. What they say and write must, therefore, sound like jargon or, even worse, like a wilful perversion of the words' 'natural' meaning.

The following passage, written by two British psychiatrists, illustrates the point. It is by no means an extreme example of its kind and, read dispassionately, it is a perfectly lucid piece of English technical prose. But, to anyone engaged on a jargon witch-hunt, it contains certain major irritants, such as 'attempters', 'personality profile', 'interpersonal behaviour' and 'intra-punitiveness'. 'Why,' such a person is likely to ask, 'must they deform the English language in this way?', ignoring the psychiatrist's protest that, to him, 'personality profile' and 'intra-punitiveness' are as necessary as 'sodium pentobarbital anesthesia' and 'elevated cholesterol levels' are to his colleagues in other fields of medicine and have as precise a meaning. He will have a very difficult task, at least in Britain – life is easier for psychiatrists in America – to convince his critics that he is much more than a highly-paid charlatan.

The quotation is taken from a discussion of the types of people who attempt suicide.

> It is generally agreed that personality disorders are common among

> those who attempt suicide (Weissman, 1974). In accordance with this was our previously reported finding (Pallis and Birtchnell, 1976) that the personality profiles of suicide attempters were significantly more deviant than those of the non-suicidal patients. The findings of the present study would appear to indicate that this deviance was contributed to largely by those who make less serious attempts. However, whereas in the previous study both male and female attempters deviated to the same extent from the non-suicidal patients of their own sex, in the present study the male non-serious attempters demonstrated the more obviously disturbed personality profile.
>
> The study of McHugh and Goodell (1971), though using a clinical assessment of personality, was in broad general agreement with the present one. It showed that non-serious attempters included significantly more abnormal personalities. It also showed them to be significantly younger. The criteria for diagnosing abnormal personality, based upon previous behaviour, were immaturity, drug or alcohol abuse, sexual deviation or promiscuity, behaviour detrimental to welfare, inability to hold job or continue with marriage, and hysterical or aggressive interpersonal behaviour. Further studies comparing the characteristics of serious and non-serious attempters are summarised in Table IV. Non-serious attempters tend to be associated with outwardly directed aggression or extra-punitiveness and impulsiveness and the serious attempters with intra-punitiveness, introspection depression, anomie and hopelessness. In three of the studies no significant associations emerged. It is difficult to make meaningful comparisons between these studies, since they utilise different populations, adopt various methods of assessing seriousness and involve a wide range of psychological tests.[24]

The law, like medicine, is a profession with a long history. Until very recently, those who practised it had followed the normal school curriculum of any educated person, that is, they had devoted many years to the study of Latin literature and of the Latin language. Much of their specialised terminology was Latin and, as lawyers, they would naturally introduce such words into their arguments and judgements as the occasion required. This interlarding of English with Latin gave legal English its peculiar flavour throughout the eighteenth and nineteenth centuries and well into the twentieth. It constituted the legal jargon and was an essential part of the equipment of the lawyers presented by dramatists and novelists, and the public expected it and laughed at it. But it is exceedingly rare nowadays. The new generation of barristers and solicitors is not at all at home with Latin and it is perfectly possible to enter the profession and succeed in it without ever having studied the language at all.

It is, however, perfectly possible to learn individual Latin terms such as 'publici jures', 'per se', 'quare' and 'consortium' without knowing any Latin, and this, in fact, is what today's lawyers do. They add the Latin words to their stock-in-trade as technical expressions, rather than as elements of the Latin language, so that their professional jargon is part Latin, part English. The effect, somewhat curious to the outside observer, is illustrated by:

> Although the action per quod consortium et servitium amisit is one of trespass and not case, damage to the husband is the gist of the action.[25]

> It makes no difference whether the animal is ferae naturae or mansuetae naturae, naturally wild or tame.[26]

> Error in negotio occurs when one party thinks he is entering into one type of transaction and the other thinks he is entering into another (e.g. sale as opposed to hire). Then there can be no contract.[27]

One can, however, read many pages of legal reports and text books without coming across any Latin words at all.

Present-day lawyers' English does, even so, possess a flavour of its own, a flavour created by the extraordinary use of ordinary words. Whether this is sufficient in itself to constitute jargon is a matter for discussion. One might begin, perhaps, by saying that, in an age in which easy, informal, colloquial, often careless English is the rule, any precise, formal style is likely to strike the man in the street as very odd. The people who affect such a style are almost certain to appear as beings from a past age, men whom history has left behind, and it could be that such an old-fashioned quality is sufficient in itself to make legal English sound and read like jargon.

At their best – and they are often at their best – judges and barristers handle English supremely well. They earn their living by doing exactly that, and by tidying up other people's loose expressions. As the Master of the Rolls, Lord Denning, put it, 'We are not the slaves of words but their masters. We sit here to give them their natural and ordinary meaning in the context in which we find them.'[28] This, however, is not as simple as it may seem. The legal context of a word is frequently, perhaps usually, not the same as its everyday context. In order to make the law work at all, lawyers are obliged to define the terms they use, to decide that in a particular context a word shall mean this and not that. Much of the work of the courts is, in fact, concerned with arguing about definitions, an activity which often strikes the outsider as either amusing or infuriating, according to his mood.

The problem is excellently set out in *Halsbury's Laws of England*:

> Most modern statutes contain an interpretation, or definition, section in which is declared the meaning which certain words and expressions are to, or may, bear or include for the purposes of the statute in question. As a rule, it ought as a matter of drafting to be used for interpreting words which are ambiguous or equivocal only, and not so as to give an artificial meaning to words the ordinary meaning of which is plain. An interpretation section does not necessarily apply in all the possible contexts in which a word may be found in the statute. If a defined expression is used in a context which the definition will not fit, it may be interpreted according to its most ordinary meaning. In practice, interpretation sections in modern statutes almost invariably contain express provision that the meanings thereby assigned are to apply unless the context otherwise requires. The fact that a particular meaning may be assigned to a term for the purposes of a particular statute by an interpretation section contained therein does not necessarily alter the generally accepted meaning of the term when used for other purposes. In the construction of an interpretation section is must be presumed that Parliament has been specially precise and careful in its choice of language, so that the rule that words are to be interpreted according to their ordinary and natural meaning carries special weight.[29]

The last sentence of this quotation is of great importance. Whatever the legal need of the moment may be, the general rule has to be that 'words are to be interpreted according to their ordinary and natural meaning'. Lawyers are entitled to make a selection from the range and shades of meaning a word can carry, but they cannot invent a meaning for themselves, according to the best authority. The Hon. Mr Justice Stamp declared in 1967:

> English words derive colour from those which surround them. Sentences are not mere collections of words to be taken out of the sentence, defined separately by reference to the dictionary or decided cases, and then put back again into the sentence with the meaning which you have assigned to them as separate words, so as to give the sentence or phrase a meaning which as a sentence or phrase it cannot bear without distortion of the English language. That one must construe a word or phrase in a section of an Act of Parliament with all the assistance one can from decided cases and, if one will, from the dictionary, is not in doubt; but having obtained all that assistance, one must not at the end of the day distort that which has to be construed and give it a meaning which in its context one does not think it can possibly bear.[30]

In this case, which involved a crematorium, the Judge refused to argue that a dead body could be held to be 'goods and materials', handled by a tradesman in the ordinary course of his business. The language used in the case reads somewhat strangely to a layman, not because it is exotic or incomprehensible, but because it assembles concepts to which he is not accustomed. He is perfectly familiar with the words 'body', 'tradesman', 'goods' and 'materials', but he is extremely unlikely ever to have thought of a crematorium or an undertaker as a tradesman or of a body as goods and materials. What he reads is therefore likely to strike him as linguistically curious, even if it does not seem to be entitled to the label 'jargon'. 'This,' he may well say to himself, 'is the strange way in which lawyers talk.'

Consider, for example, the case of the lady who brought an action against Associated Newspapers, Ltd in respect of a report in the *Daily Sketch* which said, 'Mother takes Nude's Place in Lion Show'. The lady in question, aged 22 and the mother of a baby girl, said that she had been wearing a bikini at the time, and that it was therefore libellous and a serious slur on her reputation to give the impression that she had been nude.

In his final speech to the jury, defending counsel said that

> . . . . from the point of view of the story it could not make any difference whether it was said that the plaintiff posed in a bikini. From the lion's point of view it would not matter twopence. There was every reason to think that the reporter could not have been told that the plaintiff would be wearing a bikini. He (counsel) asked the jury to say that it was rather ridiculous, monstrous, and complete nonsense for this lady, a director of her husband's company which specialized in nudes, a lady who derived her income from that company, to ask the jury for damages in respect of a statement that she had posed as a nude. The article did not say that the plaintiff posed in the nude, but that she posed as a nude. Counsel suggested that the words did not mean that she posed strictly in the nude. The jury knew that no nudes on the stage were really nude.
>
> To say of a person that she had conducted herself immodestly did not necessarily mean that she was an immodest person. Lady Godiva, who conducted herself immodestly in riding through the streets of Coventry, was certainly not a immodest woman. The defendants said that the plaintiff behaved immodestly in performing the tassel dance, but not that she was an immodest woman. If the statement that the plaintiff appeared as a nude meant that she behaved immodestly, that meant that the Quinns obtained their living by persuading girls to behave immodestly. How did the jury think the plaintiff was acting when she performed the tassel 'dance'? Dancing was not the proper word because that meant with the feet; in the tassel dance the performer remained still and the tassels revolved. Did the jury not think that that was quite obviously a decadent performance?

> If the plaintiff was entitled to damages, a packet of pins was worth more than enough to compensate here.[31]

There is no word in this passage which is not used in ordinary speech, yet the total effect is quite different from that of ordinary speech. The main reason for this is the lawyers' characteristic habit of presenting ordinary colloquial words and phrases as if they were in quotation marks, so giving the impression that the legal expert himself is standing back from the language of his fellow-citizens in order to inspect it. This allows him to remain detached and objective throughout, to be not as other men – an essential position for anyone engaged in the law. Most so-called 'legal language' consists of nothing more remarkable or unusual than this, of holding words up to the light to see if they really mean what they appear to mean. Even a preposition is not immune. To the ordinary person it may seem an immaterial piece of quibbling whether the newspaper said that someone posed as a nude, rather than in the nude, but to a court of law it is a vital point.

Of greater concern to most people, it has been necessary to seek a legal ruling on the exact meaning of 'halt', when the word is used on a road sign. In the Appeal Court, one judge said, 'I do not think there is any doubt that a car should be brought to a momentary standstill before a major road is entered'[32] and another, 'Could anything be plainer than "halt" How could a motorist halt if he proceeded stumblingly or falteringly across?'[33] Few of us would be likely to say, in the ordinary course of conversation, that a driver 'proceeded stumblingly or falteringly across' the intersection between one road and another, although we are left in no doubt as to what the judge meant. To this extent such a sentence can perhaps be said to contain jargon, forms of expression which no-one but a lawyer would be likely to use.

Examples of the same kind are plentiful, both from the work of the courts and from Acts of Parliament, which have, of course, been drawn up by lawyers particularly skilled and experienced in such matters. 'Cheese,' we learn, 'means the substance usually known as cheese, containing no fat other than fat derived from milk',[34] and 'hairdressing' means 'shaving, cutting, shampooing, tinting, dyeing, bleaching, waving, curling, straightening, setting, or dressing of the hair, upon the scalp or face, with or without the aid of any apparatus or appliance, preparation or substance; the hand or vibro massage of the scalp or face.'[35]

We have suggested earlier that several different definitions of 'jargon' appear to be in common use – specialist language which those outside a particular occupation do not understand; language which, in order to create an impression of superiority, or 'otherness', is wilfully and unnecessarily different from that used by more ordinary mortals; and language which is the necessary form of expression of people engaged in a particular kind of work. One definition inevitably shades off into another, but, in general, the first and the third type of jargon can be defended and the second cannot. It might therefore be better to reserve the term 'jargon' for the kind for which there is no reason or excuse, but it is not easy to impose this distinction, if most people do not discriminate between one form of jargon and another.

A further complication is that there is certainly something which might be called 'cumulative jargon', that is, speaking or writing which appears normal in its components, but far from normal – jargon in fact – in its total effect, after one has been exposed to several hundreds or thousands of words of it. After a lifetime on the Bench, judges understandably produce cumulative jargon almost by instinct. It is part of the air they have been breathing so long.

The following passage from a judgment by Lord Chief Justice Goddard makes the point very well:

> A finger is part of a hand. I think we have to consider not only whether a finger is an organ (within the meaning of reg. 2 (5) of the National Insurance (Industrial Injuries) (Benefit) Regulations 1948 (revoked: see now reg. 2 (5) of the National Insurance (Industrial Injuries) (Benefit) Regulations 1964)) but also whether a hand is an organ. This seems to me to be the most material thing because, if a hand is an organ, an injury to a finger is covered because the finger is part of the hand. I can understand that medical tribunals have had difficulties on this matter. I think that a layman, at any rate, would have thought of a hand as a limb and not as an organ; but we find the definition of 'organ' in the most authoritative work, the Oxford Dictionary, is 'a part or member of an animal adapted by its structure for a particular vital function, as digestion, respiration, excretion, reproduction, locomotion, perception, etc.' The dictionary goes on to give various illustrations. Locomotion would seem to include legs or feet, but it is not necessary for us to decide that. We have to construe these regulations according to the ordinary meaning of words. We have to decide the question whether or not fingers, part of the hand, are an organ. A hand is an organ; it is an organ of the human body which enables grip to be applied to any article. The hand is the prehensile part of the arm; the hand is the organ of prehension. The fingers are part of the organ of prehension because they enable a man to grip, and if a man has no fingers, he has no grip. I think, therefore, that on the face of this award there is an error in the finding that the two fingers concerned are not organs.[36]

Such masterly handling of the English language makes delightful reading, and if no-one but a judge, or a writer satirising a judge, could produce it, it may be that we shall have to label it judges' jargon.

An important point should, however, be made in any discussion of legal jargon. Lawyers, in any generation, do occasionally indulge in the habit of wrapping up a simple statement or question in a woolly mass of unnecessary and confusing words. This is probably more true of solicitors than of barristers and, where it occurs, the reason is usually carelessness or weariness, rather than any sinister intention. But a high proportion of this so-called legal jargon is generated not by lawyers, but by bureaucrats in central and local government, who are much fonder of such language and much more likely to shelter behind it than the lawyers themselves. If there has to be criticism – and eternal watchfulness is the only guarantee of a satisfactory mother-tongue – it should at least be of the right people.

No finer specimen of administrative jargon has ever appeared in English than the following, taken from the Groundnuts Amending Order of April 1956:

> In the Nuts (Unground) (Other than Groundnuts) Order the expression nuts shall have reference to such nuts other than groundnuts, as would, but for this Amending Order, not qualify as nuts (Unground) (Other than Groundnuts) by reason of their being nuts (Unground).

The officials responsible for this masterpiece would defend themselves by saying that it was of great importance that nuts and groundnuts should be kept unmistakably separate and distinct and that much trouble and expense could be caused by any confusion between the two. It is possible, even so, to believe that the result could have been achieved a trifle more elegantly.

It would be fair to say, however, that much of what is called legal English exists because there are so many dishonest and unscrupulous people in the world, lying in wait to make a dishonest penny from their fellow men. Legal documents of all kinds consequently have to be drawn up with the trickster ever in mind. There must be no word, phrase or construction which a rogue can twist and interpret to his own advantage. If it is understood, for instance, that a legally binding deed or contract must contain no commas, no criminally-minded person can change the meaning by introducing a comma in a position to suit himself. This being so, it is unfair to attack whoever drafted the document for producing inelegant, difficult to read prose. The public is in fact protected by such legal jargon as:

> Now this Policy witnesseth that in consideration of the Insured paying to the Company for this Insurance the First Premium specified in the Schedule the Company hereby agrees (subject to the condition herein or endorsed or otherwise expressed hereon which conditions shall so far as the nature of them respectively will permit be deemed to be

conditions precedent to the right of the Insured to recover hereunder) that in the event of any of the said contingencies happening. . . .

If the millenium were to arrive and if everyone were totally honest and trustworthy, this kind of jargon could be dispensed with. But only then.

2 The Politicians and the Military

'The centralised pattern of government,' Dr Alex Comfort has written, 'is today dependent for its continued function upon a supply of individuals whose personalities and attitudes in no way differ from those of admitted psychopathic delinquents.'[1] Such people have an immense appetite for power and are not likely to be scrupulous about the means they employ to gain and hold it. They will adopt the tactics and the language which seem most likely to serve their purpose.

No country, however, is governed wholly or mainly in public. The really important arguments take place, not in Parliament or Congress, but in hotel rooms, offices, private houses, the back of motorcars and on golf courses. It is here, behind the scenes and in a conversational manner, that positions are filled, favours exchanged and pressure exerted.[2] Public discussion of policies and events exists partly because of tradition and partly because it is important to obtain some token of public support for decisions which have already been taken among groups of powerful people.

This is not a new situation, nor is there necessarily anything sinister about it. Influential people tend to know one another and to mix socially. If pressure-groups did not exist, governments would be deprived of a valuable source of information about important sections of public opinion.[3] But there are certain consequences of government in private which are potentially more dangerous now than in the time of Gladstone. At any period, only a few of the men and women who influence and decide current policy are obliged to face the rough and tumble of Parliament or of Party conferences and conventions. This not altogether enviable task belongs to a specially robust and quick-witted kind of person who enjoys handling an audience and who is at home with hostility and abuse. But today there is an increasing tendency for these spokesmen, debaters, salesmen and rubber-stampers to regard themselves as a professional class. Not everyone has the peculiar combination of virtues and vices which are needed if one is to make effective use of modern methods of persuasion and publicity. Most of those who play a part in ruling England today are well content to do so from the wings, in their capacity of scientist, industrialist, financier or civil servant. They see no advantage and much discomfort in the idea of a seat in Parliament.

Perhaps the most important part of the professional politician's equipment at the present time is his capacity to regard himself as the representative of his Party, rather than as someone entitled to express opinions of his own. As a Member of Parliament he will be required to support the Party line on all public occasions. He must remember that in Parliamentary and Local Government elections the man now means almost nothing. As Robert Mackenzie has said, 'a particular candidate, whatever his merits, is not likely to add or subtract more than about 500 votes to the total his party would win in the constituency, regardless of who had been nominated.'[4]

The man of truly independent spirit has little place in modern politics. If he puts up for election without the official backing of one of the major parties, he will almost certainly lose his deposit. If he disagrees with the party leadership or if he resigns on a point of principle, his career is likely to come to a quick end. 'The unforgivable, inconceivable offence is to vote in such a way as to let the other side in. Even the killing of innocent people (including British troops), the deception of friends, the sullying of national honour, and the loss of vast material interests, are preferable to the return of a Labour government.'[5] And, from the Labour point of view, an equivalent catalogue of shame would have to be preferred to the continuance in office of a Conservative government. However much individuals may privately lament such a situation, the great majority come to terms with it, convinced, apparently, that the other side represents antichrist and disaster or, more seriously, lack of opportunity to exercise one's own talent. 'Discipline' and 'loyalty' have become the keywords in party politics.

Such cynicism and opportunism are the result of a deadening state of equilibrium between the voting strength of the Conservative and Labour parties. With such a narrow margin between winning and losing power, the slightest hint of unorthodoxy or defection is castigated as treasonable. It may well be that men are boldest and most outspoken when they can see no immediate opportunity of acquiring power or, on the other hand, no serious danger of having to give it up. The British Labour movement illustrates this very well. For fifty years, from the founding of the Independent Labour Party in 1893 until the General Election of 1945, Britain as a whole benefited a great deal from a left-wing determination to state the facts about working-class life and to demand justice for exploited people in all parts of the world. The main energies of the Labour Party went in this direction and not towards the perfecting of the Party machine. Had the machine been of the modern streamlined, all-demanding type the Labour Governments of 1924 and 1929 would have been better organised, better acquainted with the facts of political life and better equipped for survival. But as a condition of this, British Socialism would probably have lost its soul at an earlier date. So long as its discipline and organisation remained loose, it produced some interesting thinkers and writers. Such people have been misfits in the Party shadow-boxing and witch hunts which have characterised political life since 1945, and which have produced a jargon to match.

For thirty years at least, the Parliamentary Labour Party has been a far from easy body to hold together. Its members have no obvious common interest nor, so far as these mysteries are revealed to an outside observer, any common ideology. In default of these bonds all may be presumed to see the same common enemy.[6] When this too fails, the Party Whips take over and impose cohesion and discipline from without. The resulting atmosphere is hardly likely to encourage either boldness of thought or vigour of language. It fosters the professional politician, the man who thrives on circumspection andgrows fat on clichés. It blunts the enthusiasm or breaks the heart of the man or women who finds tactics a poor substitute for ideals.

Politics, it may be said with much reason, is not a suitable activity for anyone with ideals or strong principles. But it is an excellent field of operations for people with a well-developed dramatic sense and an interest in the oddities and complexities of human behaviour. Both the Conservative and the Labour Parties are, from a social and educational point of view, much less homogeneous than they were half a century ago. There are significant changes to be noted, too, in the character of the people who are to be governed. No politician can use the same form of address to an electorate which he knows contains nearly 100 per cent of the adult population as he would think appropriate to an electorate of only a little over a million people (the figures in 1866). Voters who are, in general, propertied, educated and leisured would be spoken to more or less as social equals. During the past half century politicians have had to learn the new and very difficult art of talking effectively to millions of people who have relatively little property, have received only a very basic kind of education and have quite a lot of leisure. The language of politics has had to change in order to meet this new and exacting demand. It has not always changed for the better.

Perhaps the most remarkable sign of the revolution is the decline in the prestige of the formal speech. The great speeches of the pre-1914 period were made nearly as much to be read as to be listened to. The newspapers had the pleasant habit of reporting them in full, but the reports were often so long that only a tiny proportion of the new electorate could possibly read them. The mass-circulation newspapers of the early twentieth century were willing to offer their readers the highlights of politicians' speeches but saw no point in giving them more.

Today the politician with an instinct for advancement and self-preservation is fully aware of the inability or unwillingness of the mass of the people to read his speeches, wherever they may be made. He knows that the press will ignore, compress and sensationalise what he says. He realises that if he talks directly to people on television he must be conversational, not rhetorical. At the same time, however, his experience teaches him that oratory is a useful weapon to have in reserve for Parliament or a Trades Union meeting. The result is that if he is to be successful today the politician has to be a much more flexible speaker than he needed to be in 1900. If the modern politician is exceptionally grand and important, some of his speeches may be reproduced in pamphlet form, so giving him a double return on his investment of time and thought. This is likely to produce a curious mixture of the written and spoken styles, something which is neither good listening nor good reading. There may be unfortunate consequences, too, in that material which appeared adequate in a meeting hall may be seen to have serious defects when it is exposed to the careful scrutiny and reflection which print makes possible.

Consider, for example, two speeches made during 1973 by Harold Wilson, who was Prime Minister at that time. The first, called *Individual Choice in Democracy,* was delivered at an East of Scotland Labour Party meeting at Leith on 20 January, and the other, *Democracy in Industry,* at the North West Regional Conference of the Labour Party on 17 March. Both were subsequently reprinted as pamphlets, No. 1 and No. 3, in what was known as the Edinburgh series of policy speeches.

Pamphlet No. 1 contains these two paragraphs:

> That redundancy notice, as like as not, was the result of a smart deal, where some very slick young man saw a chance of buying a mixed enterprise; with perhaps millions more pounds to make – for him, not for the community, not for the national welfare – by developing and rack-renting the property value, than by keeping even a viable factory going. So someone gets a new office block to house the new financial bureaucracy, some small shopkeeper quits to make way for a higher-rented shop charging higher prices, a factory producing a saleable product and providing a community with work is dismantled, and the machinery sold. And there's one more unit on the impersonal tally of seasonally adjusted wholly unemployed, who probably knows as little about the techniques of asset-stripping as Mr. Heath cares about the fact that it is an integral part of the system of society he has created.
>
> What he feels is that there is something cruelly unfair, morally wrong about an economic system so motivated. And our task as Socialists is not only to tell him that he is right, but that there is a choice open to him. His democratic choice, not that of some brash puppy in the City, or some tired old accountant who cannot, any more than a Tory Chancellor, see beyond the flat two-dimensional limitation of his cost-benefit analysis.[7]

And in Pamphlet No. 3 we find, in a completely different context:

> Take the redundancy notice, destroying, at a stroke, the family's security and plans for the future. As like as not it was the result of a smart deal, where some very slick young man saw a chance of buying a mixed enterprise; with perhaps millions more pounds to make – for him, not for the community, not for the national welfare – by developing and rack-renting the property value, than by keeping even a viable factory going. So someone gets a new office block to house the new financial bureaucracy, some small shopkeeper quits to make way for a higher-rented shop charging higher prices, a factory producing a saleable product and providing a community with work is dismantled, and the machinery sold. And there's one more unit on the impersonal tally of seasonally-adjusted wholly unemployed, who probably knows as little about the techniques of asset-stripping as Mr. Heath cares about the fact that it is an integral part of the system of society he has created.
>
> For the individual, for his family, the conclusion is burned into him that there is something cruelly unfair, something morally wrong, about an economic system so motivated. And our task as Socialists is not only to tell him that he is right, but that there is a choice open to him. His democratic choice, not that of some City gentleman or some tired old accountant who cannot, any more than a Tory Chancellor, see beyond the flat two-dimensional limitation of his cost-benefit analysis.

The two passages are almost identical. The manufacture of a Prime Minister's speeches has clearly become something of a scissors-and-paste job, with every brilliant phrase deserving a repeat performance. But are the phrases in fact so brilliant? Sir Harold was a considerable master of the art of getting applause for a piece of jargon which appealed to the heart, rather than to the head, and his speeches are well-supplied with such expressions as 'a glib PR-man', a 'virile democracy', 'a bureaucrat with a redundancy list', 'some very slick young man', 'the new financial bureaucracy', 'some City gentleman', 'some tired old accountant'.

It is perhaps not quite fair to relegate Sir Harold's metaphors to the level of jargon, although a great many of them, like those of other politicians, perform the function of jargon. He has been much given to using epigrams and figures of speech to confuse and demolish his opponents and occasionally his metaphors are sharp and good, if not in the first class.[8] One recalls with pleasure sentences like, 'I could not understand how any man could have a slipped disc whom Providence had failed to provide with a backbone'. Not infrequently, however, he uses metaphors in such a way as to cause his listeners to think he is saying something striking and important, when closer examination makes it clear that this is not the case at all.

There are, for example, his favourite cricketing metaphors:

> The Government have been enjoying for the past three years a batsman's wicket and now the batsman's wicket is crumbling a bit. The Chancellor's own reputation as batsman is due far more to the wicket than to his ability in using the bat. Indeed, now that the Chancellor is discarding it during this period, by dismantling controls and deciding to throw away his bat altogether and rely on his pads, I would remind him of the fate of the five English batsmen, in the first innings in the Test Match which ended today.

Even Sir Harold's most fervent admirers might well find it difficult to say just what this meant, which puts the passage very close to jargon.

When we compare the character of Parliamentary work today, both in the House and in the constituencies, with what it was before the First World War, the greatest difference, apart from the tightness of modern party discipline, is probably to be found in the pressure of duties. Members are not infrequently called upon to sit throughout the night. In each Parliament since 1950, anxious Whips have had their flocks brought into the Division Lobby on stretchers and in bath chairs and returned to hospital when the vote was safely over. Members become tired and stale and it is very natural that they should relapse into jargon, a form of language which demands the minimum of effort.

Few MPs nowadays can find time to prepare the carefully drafted and rehearsed speeches which were common before 1914. The most that a member can hope for now is reasonable accuracy in his facts and fair coherence in his presentation of them. Even if the public wanted it, oratory would be difficult to achieve under such conditions of work.

Very much more Parliamentary business is conducted in Committee now than was the case thirty years ago, and committees dislike oratory. The need is to get through the agenda as quickly and efficiently as possible and the man who orates or who gives the impression that he thinks time is of no consequence is a nuisance.

It is clear that the modern Member of Parliament will be driven, in self-defence, to discover methods of organising his work which will at least keep him out of hospital or the grave. If this were the only factor to consider, long-windedness and vagueness would have disappeared years ago. Unfortunately, there are other forces which pull the politician in an opposite direction and encourage him to hold on to habits which common sense suggests he should abandon.

One of these forces is the fact that everybody, politicians included, is living in a desperately insecure world. Not all of the insecurity depends on fear of war and of extermination. Much of it arises from such features of our lives as the difficulty of saving money or the dread of unemployment or the housing shortage or the feeling that one's social privileges are slipping away. In such a situation, a person with political ambitions may well come to believe that a successful career and strict attention to the truth do not always mix. Given such a conflict, the truth must be sacrificed.

To accuse a politician of lying is somewhat superficial. It is more useful to enquire why he is lying or half-lying. There are few ambitious men in public affairs who have not been able, at some time or other, in some cases frequently, to persuade themselves that the end justifies the means. For the good of society, the party must be kept in power at all costs, the policy must be forced through. Language is merely a tool which, skilfully handled, will ensure success.

In 1962 Arthur Sylvester, then the United States Assistant Secretary of Defense, revealed that news 'generated' by the American Government had been used with considerable success during the Cuban crisis. The Government, he said,[9] would continue to use 'news' to further its foreign policy. News, he said, was 'a weapon in the American arsenal', he added, perhaps a trifle rashly, 'I think the inherent right of the Government to lie to save itself when faced with nuclear disaster is basic.' The point has rarely been made in quite so outspoken a manner.

It is interesting and perhaps encouraging to observe that the world's most eminent futurologist, Herman Kahn, a man in continual contact with politicians and defence experts, has remained to a remarkable extent uncorrupted by their jargon. This is partly, no doubt, the result of a well-developed business sense. If one is to earn a good living by making people's flesh creep, it is as well that the ordinary man and woman should understand what one is saying. By inventing one's own jargon, or perhaps it would be fairer in this instance to say specialised terminology, and by using it in very small doses, a prophet like Kahn can have the best of both worlds. He can communicate to a wide range of people and, at the same time, enjoy the prestige that comes from the judicious use of high-priestly language. It is a very brilliant achievement. Too much jargon, and he loses touch with his public. Too little, and he descends to their level.

This passage, from his book, *Thinking About the Unthinkable*, illustrates the method.

> Let us now consider the game of chicken (or strike) in the context of an Escalation Ladder. It is useful to consider a hypothetical escalation that goes through each rung in turn; in a significant sense the scenarios summarized in the following discussion provide the background and environment for much of our negotiation and jockeying vis-à-vis the Soviets.

> *Subcrisis Disagreement*
>
> The first stage of our Ladder deals with the difference of opinion that arises between two antagonists. At this point they may still be polite to each other, but one or both sides introduces the possibility that, unless the other is reasonable, there will be a 'crisis'. It may well be said that a subcrisis disagreement between the Soviet Union and the United States has existed ever since the American Ambassador to Moscow, in 1942, publicly complained that the Soviets were not giving credit domestically to the aid they were receiving from the U.S. in the conduct of the war against Hitler. Since then, the subcrisis situation has been chronic, punctured, as it were, on a dozen occasions by higher steps on the Escalation Ladder. The essential element of the subcrisis disagreement is that both the American and the Soviet populations and governments believe that there is essentially nothing wrong with the world, and the international situation in it, except that the other side exists and pursues goals which interfere with 'peace' and their own legitimate active and passive aspirations. This though has taken hold firmly, at least in the United States and probably in the Soviet Union. In brief, it is the American consensus that so long as the Communist party rules in the Soviet Union, regardless of what its leaders do or say, there is a subcrisis.[10]

'Escalation Ladder' and 'subcrisis disagreement' may be jargon, but it is intelligible jargon, which, on the whole, helps rather than hinders the argument. One cannot say the same about the instruction given to United Nations troops and officials in Cyprus to stop using the word 'looting' in connection with the seizure of private property by the Turkish authorities and soldiers in the island.[11] The order was questioned, understandably, by the Austrian unit based in the south of Cyprus, 'where Turkish troops have for more than a year been observed taking thousands of pounds worth of Greek-Cypriot property from houses in lorries', and by Swedish officers in the Famagusta area, who 'spoke of the removal of furniture, house-fittings, cars, motorcycles and even speedboats by Turkish Cypriots under the command of Turkish Army officers'.

The Turkish-Cypriot leader, Mr Denktash, denied that any looting had taken place and assured the United Nations officials that all this property was merely being 'confiscated' and 'taken for storage', and that it is 'being accounted for'. The United Nations accepted Mr Denktash's version of what had been happening and ordered the word 'looting' to be dropped from the vocabulary of everyone in its service. The whole matter has now become a classic in the history of political euphemism. One has only to substitute 'storage' for 'looting' and peace and friendliness reign, except, of course, among the unfortunate Greeks, whose property has been stolen, whatever diplomatic word is used to describe the process.

Euphemisms may sometimes be used by politicians and military men to soften a piece of unpleasant news, but they are also a means of deception. The story is told of an angry American Air Force colonel who once complained to reporters, after a raid on Cambodia, 'You always write it's bombing, bombing, bombing. It's not bombing. It's air support.' Another piece of cover-up language used during the Vietnam war was 'It was necessary to destroy the village in order to save it.' The former President Nixon was an expert in using language in this fashion. When the war in Vietnam was being stepped up, he referred to 'pacification'. Other famous Nixonisms were 'containment', for concealing information, and 'I misspoke myself,' meaning that he had lied.

Military affairs are no longer merely the concern of the military or of government ministries specially occupied with such matters. Universities have departments devoted to examining military strategy and military history, large numbers of scientists and technologists are wholly or mainly concerned with the development of new military techniques and equipment and quickly learn to speak the language of their paymasters, futurologists add military jargon to their working vocabulary. The attitudes and forms of expression of the army and the air force are built into the life and pattern of thinking of important sections of every advanced country. Military jargon is power jargon, and, as such, has a high prestige.

Like every academic élite, the élite that makes military affairs the reason for its existence needs its own specialised vocabulary, partly to enshrine certain professional concepts and habits of mind and partly to keep the general public mystified and at a distance. Since 1945, this development of military jargon, at least in the West, has been almost entirely American. The Americans have been the big spenders on military equipment and, particularly in Vietnam, have been engaged in warfare on a major scale for a considerable part of the post-war period. It is therefore not surprising that the modern military vocabulary of the English-speaking world should have been based on American methods of creating new words. Verbs are made to serve as nouns, hyphenated nouns such as counter-city, para-military and test-ban, are coined in great profusion; established, general words, such as missile are given new and more specific meanings; and everyone who has to earn a living by keeping in close contact with military people or relevant government departments is compelled to learn a formidable series of abbreviations and initials.

There is a remarkable paradox in all this. Side by side with the euphemisms, one finds language of extreme directness and brutality.

An American manual of hand-to-hand fighting, published during the Second World War, contained the following instructions:

Eye-gouging: Best accomplished by placing a thumb on the inside of the eye-socket and to the nose and flicking the eyeball out towards the edge of the cheek.

Lip-tearing: Hook your thumb in the corner of the mouth and tear towards the corner of the jaw.

Kicks to kill: After your opponent has been downed, the kill can be made with a kick . . . It is best to be wearing heavy boots.

This is the world in which we live. It was not the world of 1900. It is a world in which eye-gouging and lip-tearing are dealt with calmly and scientifically and which has come to approve of a training which specifically rejects all moral implications of such actions for the individual. 'So far as its medical effects are concerned,' wrote a Harley Street doctor to *The Times* (14 July 1952), 'a napalm bomb is certainly not a unique agent. It is one of a group whose effect has been to increase the thermal hazard of warfare markedly during each of the wars of this century. Unlike an atomic explosion it does not cause genetic effects and is in that respect a less severe weapon.'

What is so peculiarly sinister is the degree to which the language of the manual of hand-to-hand fighting resembles that of the St John's First Aid manual:

> Using the left hand for the right artery, and vice versa, grasp the neck low down, placing the fingers behind the shoulder and the thumb on pressure point 5 immediately above and behind the collar-bone in the hollow between the muscles attached to the bone. Press the thumb deeply downwards against the first rib, which is beneath the collar-bone at this spot.[13]

The language of mercy and of wickedness have become interchangeable. The effect of the eye-gouging extract and its fellows is that of a Black Mass, said for a perverted civilisation in decline. Some of us may still retain the capacity to be shocked at the total absence of moral feeling which such language reveals and at the appalling nature of a society which permits its citizens to be trained in such methods. Yet there is a problem of government here. One section of society has to be trained in methods which must not be revealed to its fellow citizens. The public which demands and welcomes victories cannot be allowed over-realistic descriptions of the training of its own troops, or its morale will suffer. The successful prosecution of a modern war required a careful blend of euphemism and frankness. It is the supreme challenge to the public relations expert. But since the days of the Crimean and the Boer Wars the situation has changed in one important respect. What may be described as the Hemingway-cum-surgical description of suffering and violent death has become a normal feature of our lives because, first with conscription and then with the modern form of military diplomacy, peace and war shade off into one another. Nobody is immune, although for most of the time we hardly realise the new 'realism' for what it is. Here is a passage from a BBC report, broadcast at the time of the Korean War by a reputable and responsible journalist:

> One unlucky civilian – probably a Korean fisherman – did come out of doors and start peering about. I suppose he heard something. There was no need to kill him. It was quieter, anyway, to knock him out. Man, including man in a green beret, especially under the compulsion of war, is a strange mixture of impulses and sentiments. The marine who dealt with this civilian showed me, later on, the teeth-marks on his rifle-butt. 'I was sorry to have to do it,' he said 'but he oughtn't to have been there'. He added that he had dragged the unconscious man to a place where he would be sheltered from the big explosion due in an hour or so.[14]

Winston Churchill spoke much truer than he knew when, in 1901, he told the House of Commons that 'the wars of people will be more terrible than those of kings'. Most people show little resentment or disgust at the cold objective description of horrors which would have appalled the Victorians.

One reason for this is that the public is never allowed to get out of practice. It is kept in sound training during peace-time by the language of the sporting journalists and commentators. This kind of language has been bellowed into people's homes for many years.

> . . . he brings the blood from the Englishman's face; and again a rasping left jab there to the mouth, and again one there, and again one there as Woodcock comes over now, his face covered in blood, but Savold still sticks out and there is a tremendous cut over Woodcock's eye – a tremendous cut over Woodcock's eye now and Woodcock's got his face as badly full of blood as the previous fighter had by Kevitsky. How Savold is going after his man: a smashing left straight to the point of the chin there; Woodcock now fighting his way hard – a left-right and this time Savold catches him with a left hook to the face; and that eye is hurting Woodcock now, you can see him blink every time Savold comes in, Woodcock absolutely dripping with blood now; a smashing left again from Savold, and the American is cutting loose, the American is really cutting loose. Woodcock is throwing a tremendous game; left and right to Savold's face; in comes Savold again; now Woodcock's fighting the blood from his face, the American is absolutely unmarked – Savold is cutting into Woodcock, his face is just like a Red Indian's. . .[15]

The newspapers are no more reticent than the BBC:

> Marciano has an inch-long gash over his left eye, Charles' face, subject to thunderous and club-like punishment for 15 searing rounds, resembles nothing so much as a mashed-up chocolate with a strawberry centre, his chief wounds being a split right eye and a blood clot under his left cheek.[16]

This is solid food on which to nourish callous and sadistic tendencies. Millions love it and its conditioning effect is of some social importance. War, even modern war, becomes merely the continuation of sport by other means, an unusually good prize-fight, with exceptional opportunities for the commentator. In a money-worshipping world, the fabulous financial rewards earned by a handful of pugilists gives prestige to their activities. Even, or perhaps it should be particularly, women find it entirely possible to watch these gladiatorial shows without the least repulsion.

Only the actual death of one of the combatants is missing. With that detail supplied, the enthusiasts could feel that they had been given a truly Roman show. In fact, death does occasionally occur after the performance, when the victim is safely hidden away in hospital. It is not unreasonable to suggest that there has been a close link between the language of these descriptions of boxing matches and the language of the writer or broadcaster during wartime. One makes the other more possible, acts as the dress-rehearsal for it, provides training.

Modern warfare seems to have had a twofold and apparently contradictory influence on English. One form of pressure has driven it in search of the soothing, veiling phrase, the other has moved it towards stating the bald, gouging-out-the-eyeballs kind of truth. It is quite possible that the first kind of language meets the needs of the civilian population, whose chief fear is of death, and the second serves to stiffen the morale of the military, which, so far as its less experienced members are concerned, has certain inhibitions and worries about killing. Death fears and killing fears do not necessarily call for the same linguistic treatment on the part of those whose business it is to control the morale of large numbers of people.

For the civilian section of the population, it has been found a relatively simple matter to make war tolerable when it takes place a suitable distance away. It is, however, very difficult to produce an impression of dignity and efficiency when the reality consists of a bomb on the next house but one and a severed leg lying about in the garden. Publicity can do its best, but a casualty on the home front has the unpleasant habit of presenting itself to the mind and ear as a mess with very little of the heroic about it. Once war has arrived on the doorstep, whether in Northern

Ireland or in Vietnam, the propagandists are faced with some awkward problems to solve.

We have quoted examples of the 'scientific language' created for the benefit of the actual performers and spectators. Those who listen and read at a distance are more likely to learn that 'The 15th North Korean Division has been destroyed, and the remnants, perhaps fewer than 600, are now being dealt with in a pocket near Kogyon Myon.'[17] 'Destroyed' and 'dealt with' carry a vague suggestion of rats or mice. Only the exceptionally obstinate and imaginative person will translate these expressions into the crude words which allow him to get some picture of the butchery which formed the original stuff of the communiqué. Very few readers or listeners will try to probe behind the curtain of 'saturation bombing', 'weakening morale', 'neutralizing a gun emplacement', and all the other phrases which allow a bloody horror to be described as if it were a laboratory experiment.

In the sixteenth century war reporting was less sophisticated. George Gascoigne, for instance, described the siege of Antwerp in the following terms:

> I list not to reckon the infinite number of poor Almains who lay burned in their armour. Some of the entrails scorched out and all the rest of the body free. Some their head and shoulders burnt off; so that you might look down into the bulk and breast, and there take an anatomy of the secrets of Nature. Some standing upon their waist: being burnt off by the thighs. And some no more but the very top of the brain taken off with fire; whiles the rest of the body did abide unspeakable torments.[18]

Excessive euphemism and excessive realism both have a similar weakening effect on the language. One undermines its vigour, the other exhausts it, but the final result is the same. Language becomes tired and discouraged, steadily less capable of achieving its highest possibilities. One could put this another way by saying that the poetry of life is overwhelmed by the pseudo-poetry of twentieth century war. Despite the exaggerated praise lavished on it, much of Sir Winston Churchill's wartime rhetoric was pseudo-poetic, pseudo-biblical jargon, which spread a romantic veneer over the crude beastliness of war.[19]

> The Army of the Nile has asked and it was given. They sought and they have found. They knocked and it has opened unto them.

> All is over. Silent, mournful, abandoned, broken, Czechoslovakia recedes into the distance.

In North Africa we builded better than we knew.

He must indeed have a blind soul who cannot see that some great purpose and design is being worked out here below, of which we have the honour to be the faithful servants.

Poetry is creative simplification. Propaganda, by its very nature, is over-simplification, and the words which express or conceal violence eventually come to have a deadening effect on the people who listen to them or read them. A constant straining towards the heroic or towards the refined portrayal of brutality can exhaust and destroy the power of language. There is, of course, a school of thought which believes that peace is a synonym for apathy and mental deadness and that war has a beneficial effect on people's minds.

In his *Dictionary of Forces' Slang, 1939-45,*[20] for instance, Eric Partridge suggests that there is something exceptionally lively about the language of servicemen. He says, 'In the Services, at all times but especially during a war, the men live – at any rate they should live – a fuller, more exciting life . . . Such conditions of life, such activities, such stirring adventures lead inevitably to a rejuvenation, a refreshment, a tonic bracing of language. They lead also to vividness and vigour and picturesqueness.'

It is very doubtful if this is true. Compared with the monotony of their peace-time existence, servicemen might theoretically be held to live 'a fuller, more exciting life', but few of them really do, at least to anything like the extent that Mr Partridge seems to think. Long periods of sheer boredom cancel out very effectively most of the supposedly rejuvenating effect of service life, however much nostalgia there may be for it afterwards.

The theory, none the less, is an interesting one: that if a man undergoes 'tonic bracing', his language will too. This should make the language of professional athletes, or polar explorers, really scintillating, but is it? The tendency is just as likely to be towards a caste jargon, which forms part of the mystique of the job and which is stuffed with clichés and abbreviations and is exceedingly boring.

Some parts of Mr Partridge's argument are reasonable enough. It is correct to say, as he does, that 'the corporate life favours the growth of slang', and that 'Both in the war of 1914-18 and in that of 1939-45, the Combatant or Fighting Services produced a slang much richer than that used by civilians, as no doubt they did in the Napoleonic wars, the Boer War and others.'

Very few expressions, however, pass from the warriors into the permanent keeping of the British public as a whole. Four sample pages chosen entirely at random from Mr Partridge's own dictionary illustrate this. Page

A contains fourteen expressions, of which one has been absorbed into the language of civilians. Page B has twenty-one and none has gone further. On page C two out of seventeen have found a civilian appeal and on page D, none, out of twenty-one. Only 4 per cent of these 'vivid' and 'vigorous' words have been thought to be worth adopting by those out of uniform. The jargon fades away with the circumstances that produced it.

It is very easy to be deceived by the obscene and the exotic, neither of which is necessarily a synonym for the vivid and the vigorous. The language of troops is certainly obscene above the national average, but the obscenity is very unoriginal and monotonous and only exciting to anyone who has lived the kind of sheltered life which nowadays one would hardly think possible.

But whatever we may feel about battles and air-raids as a spur to fine language and original speech, war has always offered an exceptional opportunity to the jargon-mongers, the people who believe they were born to make rousing speeches and write fervid articles. The emotional content of public life is raised to a much higher level in war-time. But it has been normal, from an historical point of view, to drop into a quieter pattern of living once the war is over. Unfortunately, however, this has hardly been possible anywhere in the world since 1945. The continuing international tension has prevented the customary fall of political blood-pressure from taking place. With the atmosphere poisoned by the struggle between the Communist and non-Communist halves of the world, life still has to be lived at a high emotional pitch, attempts have to be made to revive flagging enthusiasms, a degree of heroic sternness has to be injected into populations which yearn for a rest. A state of perpetual war, even if it is only a cold war, is fairly certain to dull people's sensibilities. Under these conditions language functions as a habit-forming drug, under whose influence the mind is never fully awake.

Writing in 1938, Mr Wickham Steed was convinced that the 1914-18 war had weakened the British people's ability to concentrate:

> Certain it is that the British public has never quite regained the power of sustained attention which it possessed in pre-War years. During the war, when the public mind underwent long periods of strain, newspaper readers lost patience with any statement or piece of writing that they could not take in at a glance. They were elated one day, downcast the next, half-reassured the day after, and then again hopeful or dejected. A student of the British Press from, say 1916 to 1922, would be struck by the gradual shortening of newspaper and review articles, and by the substitution of notes or brief paragraphs for the longer disquisitions of earlier years.[21]

The willingness and ability to deal with reasoned, carefully constructed prose decreased steadily between 1918 and 1939. The Second World War speeded up the process. Reason and emotion push a person in different directions and most people need little to persuade them to respond to their emotions rather than to their reason. Moreover, in war-time nearly everybody has to get used to doing things in a disconnected fashion. Disturbances are frequent and it is difficult to secure the time or the physical conditions which make it possible to put forward a steady, continuous mental effort. But it has never been easy, war or no war, for working people to achieve such conditions. Many soldiers, particularly prisoners-of-war, have found that war gives them opportunities for relection and study which they had never been able to get previously. It is among the middle and upper classes that conditions become obviously worse.

What matters even more is the everlasting movement that war seems to bring, the vastly increased feeling of being busy, the breaking down of the normal time sense, the general fluidity of everything. Impressions come to the mind in a jerky, kaleidoscopic fashion. Fixed points of reference disappear. Anything seems possible. It is the Kafka-element of wartime which produces the lowered ability to concentrate. The dictatorships, of course, know this state of mind all the time. They deliberately and as a matter of policy offer no fixed points by which the mind can get its bearings. Everything is deliberately kept in a state of flux, in order that public opinion can be swung rapidly from one pole to another.

The democracies have not been immune from this process to the extent which is often claimed. Given the right choice of emotional words, the British or the American public can be persuaded to adopt some very rapidly changing and contradictory attitudes.

Perhaps the most curious – and the saddest – aspect of this apparently limitless capacity of both leaders and led to bewitch themselves with their own words is found in our attitude to events abroad, where self-justification finds splendid pasture in which to grow fat. During the past fifty years, for instance, British governments have found themselves faced with insurrections in every part of their former Empire. The political speeches and the newspaper articles relating to these rebellions have shown a remarkable sameness. The citizens of those countries who happen to be protesting vigorously and violently against British rule have always been 'bandits', 'terrorists' or 'gangs'. In every case, the 'forces of law and order' have eventually been obliged to hand over power to the 'terrorists' who, in a matter of months, are mysteriously transformed into foreign gentlemen with whom we have diplomatic relations in the ordinary way. And with each new country, the same tactics and the same jargon start all over again. The British, as their propaganda makes clear, are always in control of a country, for the subject people's own good.[22]

But, in Great Britain, throughout this last half-century of wars, political upheavals and new methods of manipulating masses of people, we have been spared one of the more unpleasant kinds of linguistic madness. The influence of Marxism upon it has been very small. The British Labour Party has not been built up on a basis of Marxism. 'I would sooner have the solid, progressive, matter-of-fact, fighting Trade Unionism of England than all the hare-brained chatterers and magpies of continental revolutionists', declared Ben Tillett at Bradford in 1893 and that attitude, broadly speaking, has been maintained.

The Marxist-Communist jargon is to be found, of course, in its English versions, but there is probably much less of it about now than there was ten years ago. English has not given a sympathetic reception to the literal translations from the Russian which have poisoned other European languages. Epithets of the 'hyena, hangman, cannibal, swinish international sharks' variety have not appealed to English people in the way they have to, say, the French. Even the *Daily Worker* and its successor, the *Morning Star*, have rarely gone in for the absurdities which have flourished on the Continent, nonsense of this type: '. . . une liste d'agitateurs hitlero-trotskyistes dite communiste-internationaliste'.

In the English-speaking world we have had, none the less, to face up to the basic vocabulary of Marxism. 'Capitalist', 'proletariat', 'petty bourgeoisie', 'reactionary' and the rest have done their best to prevent people from thinking clearly and honestly about politics, and in the process 'politics' itself has become a dirty word. 'The expression "political education",' Michael Oakeshott has pointed out, 'has fallen on evil days; in the wilful and disingenuous corruption of language which is characteristic of our time, it has acquired a sinister meaning.'[23]

There is, however, a jargon of the Left which is characteristic, if not exactly Marxist. A report of a Labour Party Young Socialists' Conference can say, for example.

> Dave Steed (CPSA and Blyth LPYS) linked the whole issue of unemployment to the strategy of the Labour Government. In place of concessions to big business, Dave called for a socialist approach combining militant actions in defence of jobs at shopfloor level with socialist measures on the part of the movement as a whole.
>
> The debate on racialism reflected the unanimous opposition of delegates to the scourge of racialism. Every speaker in the debate saw racialism as an attack on the unity of the labour movement and linked the racialist propaganda of the bosses' press, locally and nationally, to the use of racialism by the fascists of the NF and National Party whose aim is to cripple and break the power of organised labour.[24]

This is a typical piece of Left jargon at the present time, with the shortened Christian name, 'Dave', to give the correct democratic flavour – the Right usually keep to the full form of Christian names – the automatic-response words such as 'big business', 'militant action', 'shopfloor level', 'scourge of racialism', 'unity of the labour movement', 'bosses' 'press', 'fascists of the NF'.

This is computer stuff, and it is worth pointing out that it is common on the Left, rare on the Right and in the Centre. It can be written at great speed, as an assembly of stock components, and, among the faithful, it serves as a foolproof means of emotional communication. One more example will suffice.

> If the bosses plead poverty, let's open the books for inspection by trade union accountants and shop-stewards' committees – and we don't only want access to the ledgers of this or that subsidiary, but of the whole combine, to guard against shady practices like juggling the books to show losses at certain plants while super-profits are stacked up in some tax haven in the Channel Islands or in the South Seas somewhere.[25]

A command of such jargon is an essential part of the working equipment of anyone, inside or outside Parliament, who is active and ambitious in Left-wing politics. It is the mark of the true professional, who has learnt to refer with confidence to 'the pseudo-revolutionary middle-class totalitarians',[26] to 'the activity of the right wing, led by a reactionary Madison radio commentator'[27] and to those enemies of the people who are 'trailing behind the Trotskyite anti-Communist gangs of thugs'.[28] He will call a strike 'a day of protest', and express his belief that it 'marked a giant step in the determination of the working people to gain a stronger voice in the shaping of their own future'.[29]

If he is black, he will make much use of a highly specialised political jargon, realising that 'the cost of working with liberal-minded white people was too high'[30] and emphasising that any efforts white people may make to improve the conditions and prospects of blacks are nothing more than 'tokenism'.

On the whole, the nineteenth century was more honest, less prudish in the political and social terminology it used. Phrases such as 'the educated classes', the 'labouring poor', 'the superior artisans', 'persons of property' meant something definite. 'The workers', 'Capitalists', 'the underprivileged', mean next to nothing, but they are politically useful precisely because they are vague.

The politician who derives his power from a mass electorate must idealise both his own motives and those of his supporters. The point has been admirably made many years ago by Michael Roberts: 'No politician,' he said, 'will announce that his is the party of greed, stupidity and violence: he will say that he stands for enterprise, realism and energy, or for a policy which is firm, but cautious, idealistic but practical. If a policy is designed to appeal to the timid, it is a good thing to call it wise and patient, and to say that it represents long-sighted courage. A policy which is based on ignorant recklessness is called modern and scientific; a policy aimed at the exploitation of the poor is called national retrenchment, the robbery of the rich is called social justice.' 'Above all,' continues Mr Roberts, 'in a country such as Britain or the United States, a political leader must be sufficiently naive to be deluded by his own terminology without losing his skill in exploiting the great and enduring social divisions.'[31]

In the course of the comparatively mild attack of Marxism which English suffered, during the 1930s mainly, we have our share of the appropriate jargon, some of it from highly educated people who should have known better:

> In order to establish a socialist economic system it is necessary for the working-class to assume exactly that political relationship to the capitalist-class which the capitalist-class now assumes to the working-class. Within the working class there will be effective democracy, just as today there is effective democracy within the capitalist-class.[32]

This pretentious nonsense, which can produce a dangerous emotional response but leaves no sharp impressions on the mind, is not in the English tradition, and we can fortunately still laugh at it. Although intended for popular consumption, it is in fact utterly useless for the purpose of explaining the workings of politics and economics to anyone. It substitutes catchwords for analysis and fruitful generalisation. 'Capitalist-class', 'working-class', 'democratic' are nearly meaningless abstractions, that do not explain politics or economics to anybody. Fortunately, most politically-minded writers avoided them. In the year following John Strachey's book from which we have just quoted a representative passage, there appeared from the same publisher George Orwell's *Road to Wigan Pier*, in which we return to the real thing, the writing which comes from a man who has been out to investigate things as they really are, not as they seem in a library or on a political platform.

> Among people who have been unemployed for several years continuously I should say it is the exception to have anything like a full set of bedclothes. Often there is nothing that can be properly called bedclothes at all – just a heap of old overcoats and miscellaneous rags on a rusty iron bedstead. In this way overcrowding is aggravated. One family of four persons that I knew, a father and mother and two children, possessed two beds but could only use one of them because they had not enough bedding for the other.[33]

To write like this is to make politics and economics intelligible, to make people feel that they ought, as thinking and responsible citizens, to be concerned about these subjects. The task is an exceedingly difficult one, because, to most of our fellow citizens, politics and economics are very dull subjects.

Twentieth-century wars have obliged government to use language in two quite different ways. Great skill has been devoted to controlling civilian attitudes and behaviour, the essential problems being to maintain enthusiasm, prevent panic and, as Dr Alex Comfort once said 'to lead a horse to the battle without allowing it to smell too much blood'. It was during the 1914-18 war that most Western states became aware for the first time of the inescapable need to enter the field of mass information and mass persuasion. The simple, personal appeal of the successful First World War recruiting posters, with their pointed wording 'Who's absent? Is it *You*?', or 'Women of Britain say *Go*!' was discovered by the usual British mixture of intuition and trial and error. The elaborate machinery of rationing and control made it essential to give the public its instructions in a way which was as near foolproof as possible. By 1918 a lot had been learnt and the Ration Books, for example, of that year are admirably worded:

> *Instructions*
> 1. Register this card at once with your Butcher by filling in your name at "O" above and address at "E" and giving him that part of the card.
> 2. Sign your name also at "B" overleaf. Get your Butcher to enter his name and address at "C".
> 3. You can only buy Butchers' Meat, including Pork, from the Butcher with whom the card is registered. You can buy either meat or a meat meal with the card from any Shopkeeper or eating place.
> 4. Each numbered coupon represents ¼ of the week's ration and can be used only in the week to which it relates. A coupon or coupons must be torn off by the shopkeeper at each purchase.
> 5. This Card may be used only by or for the holder. On his dying, joining the Forces, or otherwise ceasing to use the Card, it must be returned at once to the nearest Food Office, or dropped in a pillar box.
>
> *Penalty for Misuse:* £100 or six months' imprisonment or both.

The British Ration Book of 1951 used a rather better display technique, but some of its wording was not as good as the 1918 version. Compare the bureaucratic smoothness of one of its instructions with the directness of (4) on the 1918 card.

> It is essential for the successful operation of the rationing system that the coupons should be either cancelled or cut out as appropriate whenever food is supplied to a consumer.

Two long wars, with years of mass unemployment between them, and the eventual establishment of the Welfare State have combined to force successive British governments and the Civil Service departments which serve them to work out reasonably foolproof methods of giving the public essential information and instructions. It would be flattering to suggest that they have always succeeded.

3 Literature and the Arts

On the lower levels, the language of bookselling has not changed a great deal for half a century. Its clichés have shown remarkable stamina. On one side of the Atlantic we receive such orders as:

> Fill your bookshelves with the most brilliantly colourful characters in English literature . . . Evil Fagin, the Artful Dodger, pathetic little Oliver Twist, the improvident Micawber, Mr. Pickwick and his friends, poor little Emily, Pip, Scrooge, and the rest of Dickens' unforgettable characters! Story after story, from his experiences and amazingly fertile mind. Dickens creates a world of larger-than-life people, whose lives you share . . . their joy and despair, hunger, fear, laughter, greed.[1]

and from the American side:–

> The World's greatest writers of fiction have all created stories that are immortal masterpieces. Works of such imaginative power that they have the force of actual experience. Works of such wit and wisdom that they illuminate the nature and the meaning of life. Works of such rich variety, that they penetrate every aspect of human existence and have become part of the literary heritage of all mankind.
>
> Now, for the first time, these masterpieces of fiction are to be published in a truly luxurious collection – forming a private library of great literature unlike any other ever published before . . . Jack London – who wrote of man and animal tested to the limits of endurance in the Arctic wilderness . . . The masters of irony, whose stories combine surprise with the overwhelming force of truth. Guy de Maupassant – whose classic stories penetrate to the very core of life. Thomas Mann – whose stories probe the essence of humanity . . . Ernest Hemingway – whose terse, colloquial, virile stories combine simplicity with overwhelming impact.[2]

Writing this kind of blurb is an industry in its own right. It has very little to do with the books it promotes and the professional talent on which it depends can be switched without difficulty to selling furniture or Caribbean holidays. Whether Dickens, London, Mann or Hemingway would have approved of their work being marketed in such a way we cannot tell. So far as the commercial world is concerned, their achievement was to have produced not good writing but saleable commodities, and they consequently qualified for the normal advertising approach to the customer.

In their lifetime, those who write, paint, sculpt, play, act and dance necessarily live in two worlds – the world of other writers, painters or whatever form of art it happens to be and the much larger and more heterogeneous world of those who are interested in these matters as consumers. Some of the consumers will have almost as much specialised knowledge as the artists themselves, others, for reasons of snobbery, will pretend to have more knowledge than is in fact the case and others will have what is clearly a surface interest. All these people constitute an artist's public. They are also the reviewer's and the critic's public, and these artistic middlemen are the spreaders of jargon as well as the purveyors of enlightenment.

An old-established publisher's trick is to lift favourable sentences and phrases from reviews and incorporate them in advertisements. One consequently finds a book recommended in such absurd terms as:

> 'A quietly passionate biography' *New York Times.*
>
> 'A truly penetrating story. Comprehensive and compelling, direct and dramatic' Louis Untermeyer.
>
> 'Deeply moving. The story of a spendid man, told simply and with a controlled affection' Irving Howe.[3]

'Quietly passionate', 'truly penetrating', 'deeply moving', 'controlled affection' are familiar clichés in the publishing world. Reviewers, including many whom one might expect to do better, churn them out with regularity and dependability. They have become part of the advertising machine, and they are not so much reviewers as writers of advertising copy. Nobody on the staff of an advertising agency could do any better for their clients than the supposedly objective and independent authors of the following:

> A totally engrossing tell-all. Few autobiographies convey so intimately what is involved in creativity.
>
> A vivid revelation of the romantic, intuitional creative spirit in action. I want everyone to love this book, and I hardly see how anyone who reads it can fail to.[4]
>
> Jacky Gillott's *A True Romance* is a perceptive, intelligent novel about personal relationships.[5]

It would be a little unfair to say that passages such as these form part of the language of literature, but they are unquestionably built into the business of producing and selling books. Even writers who would normally pride themselves on the care with which they select words and who shudder at the sight and sound of a cliché are liable to go to pieces when a review copy of a novel or a biography is placed in their hands. The process is difficult to explain. What happens, perhaps, is that the reviewer feels, consciously or subconsciously, that he must produce a fair ration of these dreadful phrases in order to help a fellow-author. He has, so to speak, a duty to provide acceptable fodder for the people who compose the publishers' advertisements, almost as a matter of religious ritual. How else is one to account for a critic such as Cyril Connolly, who prided himself on the meticulously worked-over quality of his writing and who was frankly and unashamedly a literary snob, offering to the world such an idiotic and laughable description of a book as: 'Delightful refreshing and intelligent. So cool, so collected, so analytical an arrangement of consciousness'?[6]

The situation was well described by George Orwell.

> Publishers have got to live, like anyone else, and you cannot blame them for advertising their wares, But, [he went on] the truly shameful feature of literary life before the war was the blurring of the distinction between advertisement and criticism. A number of the so-called reviewers, and especially the best-known ones, were simply blurb writers. The 'screaming' advertisement started some time in the nineteen-twenties and as the competition to take up as much space and use as many superlatives as possible became fiercer, publishers' advertisements grew to be an important source of revenue to a number of papers. The literary pages of several well-known papers were practically owned by a handful of publishers, who had their quislings planted in all the important jobs. These wretches churned forth their praise – 'masterpiece', 'brilliant', 'unforgettable', and so forth – like so many mechanical pianos.[7]

From his own experience, Orwell described how one of these unfortunate hack-reviewers worked, in a constant attempt to write something impressive about books which possessed no real merit at all, but for which public praise somehow had to be found. The hack-reviewer, with an assorted parcel of books to review.

> Blear-eyed, surly and unshaven, he will gaze for an hour or two at a blank sheet of paper until the menacing finger of the clock frightens him into action. Then suddenly he will snap into it. All the stale old phrases – 'a book that no one should miss', 'something memorable on every page', 'of special value are the chapters dealing with, etc. etc.' –

will jump into their places like iron filings obeying the magnet, and the review will end up at exactly the right length and with just about three minutes to go.[8]

The situation may not be as bad now as it was during the 1930s, but it would be untrue to say that hack-reviewing and the jargon that belongs to it are things of the past. A look at any issue of the *Times Literary Supplement, Encounter,* the *New Statesman* or the *New Yorker* will prove the contrary. If reviews contained no jargon, publishers would have no jargon to quote in their advertisements. This sort of jargon starts in the reviews and the articles. Sometimes it is simply laziness or weariness, sometimes a private language, but in either case the editor has failed his readers. He has neglected the primary duty of an editor, to ensure that communication takes place between his writers and his readers. The only defensible position is that adopted by Orwell when he was Literary Editor of *Tribune.* 'I refuse,' he said, 'to be responsible for printing anything that I do not understand. If I can't understand it, the chances are that many of our readers will not be able to either.'[9]

Orwell's view is not universally held. The editor of a highly respected periodical devoted to the visual arts told the present author that he not infrequently found the articles and reviews written by one of his regular contributors, a specialist in contemporary art, largely unintelligible. Why, then, did he print them? The reason was, it appeared, that he trusted the expertise of this particular contributor and felt obliged, therefore, to let him write what he wanted, in the confidence that the public would understand tomorrow what it found baffling or incomprehensible today.

For an editor or a publisher to trust his authors is admirable, but everyone benefits by being asked from time to time, 'Exactly what do you mean by that? It means nothing to me. Would you translate it for me, please?' This is not at all the same as insisting that everything one writes must be immediately intelligible to the meanest intelligence. All that is being asked of a writer is that he should make a genuine effort to communicate, and, where the concept is difficult, that he will try to meet his readers at least half-way. Much of what critics write is self-indulgence. They are playing around with words and pleasing themselves. It is very doubtful, in some instances, if they have an audience in mind at all. If they have, it must be limited to a few like-minded friends. Anyone is entitled to cultivate a private language of this kind but, when it is transferred to a newspaper or periodical which is bought by the general public, one is faced with what comes very close to being a confidence trick. The reputation of the author, sometimes deserved, sometimes not, may carry the swindle through, at least for a time, but a confidence trick remains a confidence trick, no matter how successful it is.

Under the spiritual, if not the official leadership of Dr F.R. Leavis, the

Cambridge English School built up a great reputation during the 1930s and 1940s. The disciples of Dr Leavis found their way into teaching, journalism and criticism and their distinctive attitude to literature and special way of expressing themselves had a wide influence, which was reflected in certain key books by Dr Leavis himself, and in two periodicals, *Scrutiny* and, later *Critical Quarterly*. For the Leavisites, only a very few authors appeared to be worth reading – D.H. Lawrence and George Eliot were particularly revered – and they developed a special vocabulary of praise and blame, which easily shaded off into jargon. 'Vital', a word taken from the blood and guts theories of Lawrence himself, was especially popular. One finds it frequently used by one of the most distinguished of Dr Leavis's pupils, Raymond Williams. Williams refers, for instance, to Lawrence's 'vital study of relationships'[10] and writes of 'the magnificent contrasting vitality of literature'.[11] With one foot in Marxism and the other in the theories of Dr Leavis, Raymond Williams has a prose style which is rooted in the two main sources of literary jargon in the post-war period, and which makes it natural for him to produce such passages as, 'The idea of culture is a general reaction to a general and major change in the conditions of our common life. Its basic element is its effort at total qualitative assessment.'[12] Phrases like 'total qualitative assessment' and 'our common life' are not in the main stream of English literary criticism, although they translate easily enough into German and Russian, or even French. The great English critics of the past have been more concrete, more discursive, more confident, more humane. 'What,' one can imagine Dr Johnson or Coleridge or Matthew Arnold saying, 'does the man mean by "total qualitative assessment" or "our common life"?'

There certainly is an English literary jargon nowadays and paradoxically, since it divides the initiated from the uninitiated, it is most commonly found among writers who pride themselves on their social consciousness and democratic spirit. Consider, for example, the following extracts from an article on the plays of Arnold Wesker. 'Wesker and his audience,' we are told, 'carry the burden of the dramatic experience together and find its coherence as an artistic statement simultaneously',[13] and later we learn that Wesker gives us 'a firmer grasp of life's exigencies and a more deliberate and purposeful sense of urgency'.[14]

This, we may well feel, is simply an academic way of swimming with the tide. The ordinary playgoer enjoys a play, but the learned critic feels obliged to bring the author into the situation, so that they can 'carry the burden of the dramatic experience together'. Why, incidentally, is it a burden? And, 'a firmer grasp of life's exigencies' is only a pompous way of saying 'a new way of looking at life's problems'. What 'a more deliberate and purposeful sense of urgency' means, God alone knows. Do Wesker's plays make an audience burn with a determination to bring down the government tomorrow or to shoot the members of the Stock Exchange?

Or simply to work harder and faster to create the New Jerusalem?

Faced with criticism of this quality, one can obtain some relief by italicising the jargon.

> The theatre has become the centre of *intense, controversial interest* and *a remarkable number of talented writers* have been quick to realise *the potentiality of the stage as a living social force.* Harold Pinter, Shelagh Delaney, John Arden, Bernard Kops and Doris Lessing are just five of these *new dramatists* who have realised that the theatre, allowing them as it does, *direct access to their public,* can be exploited as *a medium of immediate social and moral commentary.*[15]

The art world is even more richly endowed with such fashionable wordiness. Here are two examples from a single issue of the *Connoisseur.* The first relates to the paintings of Kandinsky.

> It is possible to stand before a Kandinsky of this period and after the first riotous pleasure, to pick one's way in and out of the world of forms; some too hot and violent to touch, others tranquil roadways through the heavens.[16]

The second passage comes from a discussion of the work of Barbara Hepworth.

> It seems wholly illogical that although most of Barbara Hepworth's drawings are representational, most of her sculptural oeuvre is organic. It would therefore be impossible to simplify down to the inner arresting movement if confined to chiselling a synthesis of human figuration. When art has to be fundamental no distracting detail is possible. There must only be a totality concentrated on Oneness.[17]

Both these writers, one might feel inclined to say, had space to fill and a living to earn. Whether they had anything worth communicating is difficult to say, since what the reader is offered is art jargon of the most esoteric and inflated kind. One can, if one is in the right mood, and if the picture is a good one, enjoy Kandinsky's use of colour and one can appreciate his skill in balancing forms. But to speak of 'riotous pleasure' and of forms 'too hot and violent to touch' is absurd. Kandinsky is not a great enough painter ever to show us 'the heavens', let alone to provide us with 'tranquil roadways' through them. The sentence is pure jargon, a bridge between one art-snob and another.

It is pretentious and unnecessary to refer to Barbara Hepworth's 'sculptural oeuvre', instead of her sculpture, and the use of the word 'organic' is a barrier to clear thinking. 'A totality concentrated in Oneness' should have been blue-pencilled the instant it appeared on the editor's desk. Such phrases do little to benefit the *Connoisseur's* reputation.

After one has turned this weird language upside down and inspected it from all sides, the possibility of a meaning emerges. Barbara Hepworth, the critic seems to be struggling to say, has a feeling for what is essential in the shape of the human body. In order to make sure that she communicates this, she pares away all the details which seem to her irrelevant and which could confuse the truth she is trying to present to us. And so we have shapes and forms, not bodies.

Why, one may well ask, does the *Connoisseur's* contributor not say something like this? Why does a simple statement have to be covered over with such revolting layers of fat as 'totality concentrated in Oneness'? The answer is obvious – the writer felt that something more prestigious and scholarly was required if he were to preserve his reputation and justify his fee. The jargon he wrote has a certain masonic quality about it, conveying to other ciritics that the author has been properly initiated into the art world and that he can be fully trusted to say the right things at the right times. But – and the question is all-important – for whom are the articles and reviews in the *Connoisseur* intended? If the answer is 'the international world of art-critics and mutual back-scratchers', the journal's readership is being unnecessarily restricted and it is not having the influence it might have. Jargon can be commercially dangerous, as well as offensive.

There is, however, a more sinister reason for art jargon and one should state it plainly. It increases the market value of the object to which it is attached. What is created in this way is a kind of religiosity, a mystery, surrounding the picture. Regarded from this point of view, art jargon is a priestly language and as such, fundamentally undemocratic. If the picture is without the power to speak for itself, at least in the saleroom, the priests must give it a voice.

We are therefore faced with something close to a conspiracy. The point has been well made by Seymour Slive, in the course of an interesting essay on Franz Hals. The passage is worth quoting at some length, partly for the support it gives to the conspiracy theory and partly to illustrate the fact that it is still fortunately possible to say useful and even profound things about works of art without descending into jargon.

> Images were first made to conjure up the appearance of something that was absent. Gradually it became evident that an image could outlast what it represented; it then showed how something or somebody had once looked—and thus by implication how the subject had once been seen by other people. Later still the specific vision of the image-maker was also recognised as part of the record. An image became a record of

how X had seen Y. This was the result of an increasing consciousness of individuality, accompanying an increasing awareness of history.[18]

> Yet, [he continues] the way people look at a work of art is conditioned by a number of assumptions about art which we have been conditioned to accept. These include learnt ideas about Beauty, Truth, Taste, and Civilisation, many of which belong to yesterday's world, not today's.
>
> Out of true with the present, these assumptions obscure the past. They mystify rather than clarify. The past is never there waiting to be discovered, to be recognised for exactly what it is. History always constitutes the relation between a present and its past. Consequently fear of the present leads to mystification of the past. The past is not for living in; it is a well of conclusions from which we draw in order to act. Cultural mystification of the past entails a double loss. Works of art are made unnecessarily remote. And the past offers us fewer conclusions to complete in action.[19]

Such a situation Slive rightly regards as undemocratic. The only people who benefit are those who create it.

> The art of the past is being mystified because a privileged minority is striving to invent a history which can retrospectively justify the rule of the ruling classes, and such a justification can no longer make sense in modern terms. And so inevitably it mystifies.[20]

It is significant that the remarks just quoted are not taken from the *Connoisseur* or from any other art magazine. They are to be found in a booklet published jointly by two organisations committed to the task of communicating ideas to a large, heterogeneous public. People commissioned to write for them have a duty to make themselves intelligible. Some achieve the task better than others, but it is significant that jargon, whether of the artistic or any other variety, is rare in the material the BBC publishes to accompany its broadcasts. One could put this another way by saying that many of the people employed to write books and articles for the literary and art periodicals are not really communicators at all. Their main aim is to impress, to prove that they are playing in the top league.

What, one is entitled to ask, does a critic or a reviewer, whether of a book, a concert, an art exhibition, a wine or a restaurant, imagine his business to be? What is he setting out to do? Two things can reasonably be expected of him, that he explains carefully what he has seen, read, tasted or heard and that he assesses its merit, using words which make sense to the people he imagines himself to be addressing. Any piece of writing may, of course, fall into the wrong hands, and the critic is not to be blamed for that. What can reasonably be laid against him is mere showing off and indifference to the needs and knowledge of his public. It is useful to measure what may at first sight look like jargon against these two possibilities.

Here, for instance, is part of a review of a new book about the Victorian painter, Landseer, published in what is known in the trade as ' a quality Sunday newspaper'.

> Landseer is something of a demonic paragon, summarising as he does the compounded vices of Victorian art and character. His painting has the opposing faults of fussy over-elaboration and sketchy negligence; his personality equally manages a paradoxical combination of opposing frailties – assiduous snobbery and pretentious gentility are entwined with neurotic procrastination and an eventual maniacal morbidity. The paintings may be deciphered as images of that self-disabled character; their lacquered finish is anxiously sycophantic, but their excess of sentimentality hints at a vengeful delight in cruelty.[21]

The result, if not the aim of the book discussed here, is to show that Landseer's painting was grossly overvalued in its day and that it was ripe for re-assessment and, as it happened, deflation. The reviewer makes this clear enough and obviously has considerable sympathy with his author's views. No reader of the *Observer* could fail to realise that he was in contact with yet another piece of debunking of a Victorian hero and to this extent the reviewer has faithfully reflected the purpose and spirit of the book entrusted to him. What is open to doubt, however, is whether every reasonably intelligent reader would understand, at least with any degree of accuracy, what the reviewer means by 'a demonic paragon', 'an eventual maniacal morbidity', 'that self-disabled character', 'their lacquered finish is anxiously sycophantic'. Phrases like these can be fairly described as reviewer's jargon. They occur, to some extent, because what the reviewer wants to say has to be compressed into an inadequate space. He is not given a proper chance to explain himself and the reader is saddled with far too much interpretation and guesswork as a result.

The author of a book is not subject to this pressure and he should therefore be free, at least in theory, to choose whatever words and texture he pleases. He has no need to squeeze the life out of his writing by compressing into five hundred words a sequence of thoughts that, for complete intelligibility, demands two thousand. This is not, of course, to say that art jargon, musical jargon or literary jargon occur only in short pieces of writing. Would that it were so. But books, in general, have much less of it than articles or reviews. A couple of paragraphs of vintage jargon can be merely incomprehensible or funny, but a couple of pages or chapters of it are intolerable.

One can, for example, read Sir Roland Penrose's excellent book on Picasso from cover to cover without stumbling over even the odd specimen of jargon on the way, whereas a critic let loose on a Picasso exhibition is almost certain to produce a generous ration of the phrases peculiar to his profession. Few critics would find it possible to write anything as simple and straightforward or as lacking in self-indulgence as:

> Sympathy for the violent expression and primitive strength of Negro sculpture came at a moment when Picasso was again preoccupied with the realisation of solid forms on a two-dimensional surface. His thoughts were inspired by sculpture, but it was not until two years later that he turned again to modelling. Before this happened, though he thought as a sculptor, he acted as a painter. Even in a still-life such as *Flowers on a Table,* the flowers are endowed with such solidity as to suggest the possibility of making a reconstruction in bronze. The planes, luminous with colour, are determined by strong outlines and heavy shading, a technique which suggests the fronds of a palm or the tattoed patterns on the naked bodies of Negro statues. In the large *Nude with Drapery* which is now in Russia, he combines his sculptural sense of form with a vigorous and exciting surface pattern accentuated by heavy hatching which gives the effect of light filtered by jungle vegetation.[22]

It is difficult to be a regular user of jargon and to possess a strong sense of humour. Most addicts, in all fields, tend to take themselves very seriously, from which one may be permitted to deduce that jargon is to a considerable extent a matter of temperament. The irreverent are apt to find jargon funny, but those who live by jargon are usually unable to understand what the merriment is about.

In the arts, as with any other kind of activity, one must distinguish between, on the one hand, professional language, which is the only way of expressing certain technical concepts and, on the other, the kind of nonsense language used by professionals which can and should be translated at birth. The first is not jargon, the second unquestionably is.

This, for example, is fully justified, genuinely professional language, referring to Debussy's music:

> Characteristic are chains of triads, of seventh, ninth or eleventh chords, or of related structures built on fourths or major seconds arrranged in pentatonic, whole-tone diatonic, or chromatic patterns, the last named including free, sliding chromatic shifts based on 'secondary-function' chords but often arrived at through parallel or sequential motion. This

parallel, symmetrical (rather than contrapuntal, contrary) motion has its counterpart in the rhythmic and phase structure, also built on parallelism and symmetry.[23]

And so is this:

The ending of *Makrokosmos III* now repeats the final 'ewig' of *Das Lied* a tritone higher B-flat/A flat over the tolling low fifth or G-flat, but its effect has been changed to a redeeming 'reconciliation'. The change is conveyed by the pentatonic consonance; its amplified resonance; the Mussorgsky references; the interpolation of high whole-tone clusters from Messiaen; high statements of the Bach fugue subject that, whistled and played, become whole-tone by extension, among which one thickened with parallel chords, as in Debussy, to incorporate it into a bright texture; whole-tone dithyrambs on the glockenspiel.[24]

It is of little consequence that a musically illiterate person has no idea as to what these two passages are about. If he were literate, he would understand them. But in order to understand the kind of jargon perpetrated by many of the people who earn a living from writing about music, education and literacy are not enough. The crust of words is too thick to be cracked by knowledge, or even by the very powerful combination of knowledge and faith.

Consider, for example, the kind of non-communication achieved by a depressingly large number of writers on modern music. Their language, one fears, is more often than not a reflection of the music's own total failure to communicate to anything that one could reasonably call a public. What is one to make of 'Volume refers to maximum loudness as well as to characteristic articulation of the attack-decay phenomenon,'[25] or '. . . that boundless prolixity by which everything is correlated in a way that is almost covertly polyvalent'.[26]

Anyone who attempts to write about the music of such composers as Stockhausen, Webern or Schoenberg is faced with an almost impossible task. He is required, at one and the same time, to defend and explain music which to a majority of people who read this book or article is, if they are honest with themselves, incomprehensible and quite possibly repulsive. But, since a high proportion of his readers can be counted upon to be very dishonest, he is usually on fairly safe ground. Readers and writer are parties to the same pretence with the conspiratorial language of jargon to bind them together and defend them against a hostile world. And so we have:

These songs – like many early works of Schoenberg – show an excep-

> tional sensitivity to texture, and indeed the most basic and compelling formal aspect of the composition is its underlying organisation in fluid, flashing, chromatic textures set into patterns of great severity and profundity.[27]

and

> Webern reduced the experience of sound to its essentials; he also demonstrated the possibility of an organic reintegration which evolved from universal prototypes into new and meaningful expressive structures.[28]

and

> Many of these works are built on tiny, cell-like structures which retain their essential, immovable identity through every kind of registral, rhythmic, dynamic and color shift: the larger result is an accumulation of potential energies which twist, turn, combine and recombine, destroy and reconstruct an apparently unyielding materialism. Nearly all of Wolpe's work is closely involved therefore with a complex use of the energies produced by the act of performance and, as much as anything else, it is this flow of form-making energy which gives his music its unique character.[29]

and

> Feldman created the first minimal art in the strict sense not only because of his use of simple, extended, isolated sounds but also because of his rejection of process and conflict of any kind and his insistence on the essential 'it ness' of the sound.[30]

Anyone who writes about music or the visual arts must make extensive use of metaphors, and some metaphorical expressions, including many of the best, demand considerable effort on the part of the reader. Even so, metaphors can become a little mixed, so that the result is bewilderment, rather than illumination. The following sentence is on the brink of jargon, if not actually over it.

> The Scala orchestra are marvellously responsive, warm of tone yet without an ounce of superfluous fat, so that textures are fine and clear.[31]

Here, on the other hand, is an original metaphor, which repays the effort required to understand it:

> The clearest example of a ridged silence which adheres to an incoming edge in the silent beat with which so many compositions begin.[32]

In other instances it is difficult to decide whether the writer has anything worth communicating or not. This critic seems, on examination, to be saying no more than that he thought a piece of music was exceptionally well played, with plenty of energy when required.

> The performance of Mozart's K482 Piano Concerto was among the finest I have ever heard, beautifully pellucid yet with plenty of fibre when required.[33]

'Pellucid' and 'fibre' are merely professional noises, made by someone who feels that such words are expected of him. They add nothing to the sense, or to the reader's understanding of the work.

One or two of the most frequently used examples of musical jargon are so traditional and so old-established that it is quite often difficult to recognise them for what they are. All solo performers and all conductors must, for example, be either 'young' or 'distinguished'. It is considered impolite merely to give the name, to refer to the person without the appropriate label. Broadly speaking, every soloist is 'young' up to the age of thirty-five. After that, he is expected to have become 'distinguished'. We therefore have 'The young Russian pianist, Dmitri Alexeev,'[34] and 'The distinguished French baritone's voice'.[35] To say 'the Russian pianist, Dmitri Alexeev', or 'the French baritone's voice' would be regarded as highly unprofessional.

Some critics make great demands of their readers. This passage, on close examination, would appear to be at the jargon end of the metaphorical spectrum, and to say a good deal less than it promises at first sight: 'Black tone, hypertension and a brutal forcing of the pace formed a most appealing amalgam, but it was difficult to view such a relentlessly muscular assault on the music's surface in a more flattering light.'[36] What, if anything, is 'black tone'? How can a combination of 'black tone', 'hypertension' and 'brutal forcing of the pace' possibly be 'appealing'? What is the difference between an 'assault' and a 'muscular assault'? How does one assault anybody or anything without using the muscles?

A similar piece of superficially clever nonsense is to be found in: '. . . the pianist's pre-stressed concrete hardness in the tutti . . .'[37] Pre-stressed concrete is, in fact, no harder than ordinary concrete.

The following two extracts, however, contrive to steer clear of jargon and mystification, although the first gets perilously close to cliché towards the end.

> . . . the first movement of the Fourth . . . was just tentative enough at times to make one feel that perhaps Rostropovich wanted to achieve more in the way of tension and blazing impact at the climaxes and was hampered by certain technical problems. The mystical balm of the quiet moments, though, was quite hypnotic, and elsewhere in the Symphony there were treats in plenty.[38]

> My musical language is based on the personal use of derivatives of the post-serial and micro-tonal techniques. It uses sonorous chords formed by massive columns and bunches of sound that remain suspended in the air while changing their colour and form.[39]

We come back to jargon with:

> Ten years ago, Dame Janet's first recording of *Frauenliebe und-leben,* on a bargain label, appeared as an unannounced wonder, radiant of manner, rapt with passion, candour and reticence. The remake is far more assertive, with words relished and shaped with remarkable projectile force and conviction.[40]

The critic may just possibly be quoting at the end of his first sentence. He may intend us to understand that the dreadful phrases, 'an unannounced wonder', 'radiant of manner', 'rapt with passion, candour and reticence' were used when the recording was originally issued. On the other hand, 'relished and shaped with remarkable projectile force and conviction' suggests that he himself would have been perfectly capable of putting his hand to such nonsense. How, we are entitled to ask, is anything 'relished with projectile force and conviction'? Is conviction a quality that projectiles are capable of possessing?

We may, after ploughing our way through a good deal of musical criticism, feel strongly inclined to sympathise with the authors of *The Language of Modern Music,* when they write: 'The "language" of music, in whichever sense one takes it, seems incapable of the kind of rigid conceptual "fit" which a dictionary seems to provide. It may be the case, as Wittgenstein believed, that the various forms of cultural expression cannot be explained beyond simply admitting their diverse character.'[41] Does this mean that all explanation of criticism of music and the visual arts is inevitably doomed to failure, that everyone has to find his own way and that no help from outside is possible, that one knows if something is good or bad without being able to say why, and that all attempts to build bridges of words between an artist and the public are irrelevant and absurd?

This seems unnecessarily defeatist. A good critic, that is, an honest expert sincerely trying to be helpful, can do his best to answer these questions:

1. What is the composer or artist trying to say? What is his vision and his intention?
2. What innovations or technical difficulties stand between the work and the public?
3. What impression did this work and, in the case of music, its performance, make on me, the critic, personally?

4. If music is under discussion, how effective was the performance?
5. How is the work to be placed and assessed in its historical context?

The replies to all these questions must be to a great extent subjective. The critic or reviewer must make it clear, implicitly or explicitly, that he is giving his own opinion and describing his own reactions. To use jargon is the favourite way of avoiding this prime duty. Jargon, by definition, is not a personal language. It is a screen, a blanket of words, behind which there may or may not be a real, thinking person. Keeping oneself out of one's work is a convention which has been followed by scientists for at least four generations. Scientists now, by tradition, use an impersonal style for presenting the results of their work, whatever emotions they may have felt during the course of it, and far too many writers in non-scientific fields have been impelled to imitate what they take to be the scientific approach and style. When such people are dealing with one or other of the arts, jargon is the almost inevitable result. This is what can happen when the work of a photographer is under analysis: 'On the whole, Lerner's prints have a virtuosic, rather eclectic demeanor, and what imagery there is, consisting largely of eyes and magnifying lenses, has its referents in the medium.'[42] Passing over the fact that 'virtuosic' is an unpleasant word and that, although a person can have a 'demeanor', 'style' is more appropriate to a photograph, we may enquire what virtue there is in saying 'has its referents in the medium', which is bogus science, instead of 'echoes the medium itself', or 'is derived from the medium itself'.

Often quite small changes are all that are needed to remove the jargon flavour from a piece of art criticism and to make real communication more likely. As it stands, the following passage is unlikely to win the author a very wide circle of friends. The jargon forms a barrier which few people are likely to wish to penetrate.

> Boogaert's geometrizations seem to operate on the quite tenable philosophical premise that all human perception of the external world is actually mediated by a vast network of assumptions, mental constructs and physiological operations and that this complex internal machinery is, in fact, as much a part of our view of the world as are the objects we see in it.
>
> What attests to Boogaert's increased self-assurance as an artist is that he realises that he does not need a blatantly obvious pattern or configuration to get across the idea of an imposed mental structure: it is inherent in the fact that he has broken a continuous unmarked temporality into discrete units. That the differences between the individual frames of a given contact sheet frequently lie beneath the threshold of perception does not disturb him – he is after all only reporting the results of applying a particular schema upon a natural phenomenon.[43]

Suppose, however, that one makes a few apparently minor, but in fact very significant modifications, putting 'seem to me to operate', instead of 'seem to operate', and 'conditioned by' for 'mediated by', omitting 'blatantly' and 'or configuration'. We could then substitute 'time sequence' for 'unmarked temporality' and 'separate' for 'discrete' and, after some thought, leave 'contact sheet' as a technical expression, rather than a jargon phrase. The reader is then able to get a little closer to what Boogaert is up to, although he may still turn out to be an acquired taste.

The temptation to use jargon increases as the intrinsic merit of an artistic composition goes down. If the critic believes that there are pop artists whose work and importance are on the Rembrandt level, considerable verbal feats are going to be required if the public at large is to be brought round to the same way of thinking. In such a situation, jargon really enters its kingdom. Here is an example of the talent in operation:

> The real Pop artist not only likes the look of his commonplace objects, but, more important, exults in their commonplace look, which is no longer viewed through the blurred, kaleidoscopic lenses of Abstract Expressionism, but through magnifying glasses of factory precision.[44]

The author then indulges in the old trick of knocking the reader off his balance by assuring him that pop art must be worth his attention, because it is 'aware' and 'relevant'.

> The explosion of the advertising and communication industry, and the speed with which images and information now travel through media channels have resulted in a much broader awareness and a more extended development in our total environment.[45]

After that, one can go in for the kill with a completely unjustified and immoral identification of pop art with abstract art, which conveniently ignores the fact that what may well be true of abstract art on a high level may not be true at all of abstract art on the low level of pop art, always allowing for the possibility that pop art may not be entitled to the label 'abstract art' at all.

> Abstract art has a great deal in common with those principles of modern linguistics which assert that content never has a meaning in itself, but that it is only the way in which the different elements of the content are combined together which gives it a meaning.[46]

Once this point has been reached, it is only a small step to proclaiming that no one outside the ranks of the creative artists themselves is in a position to understand and explain what an artist is attempting to do. The artistic mystery is, so to speak, in the sole keeping of the people who produce the art.

> In the early 1960s [writes one historian of the period] the functional separation of theory and practice – the former being the province of critics, philosophers and art historians, the latter being the concern of artists – was still accepted without question. By mid-decade, however, certain artists (those associated with Minimalism) realised that making explicit the theoretical basis of their art was too important a matter to be left to non-artists, no matter how sensitive and sympathetic, and they began to annex the role of the critic. In the 1970s their successors have assumed total responsibility for elucidating the theory underlying their practice.[47]

This would appear to put the professional critic permanently out of business, which might well produce more jargon, not less. The producers of incoherent, incomprehensible, self-indulgent paintings and musical compositions are hardly likely to be able to explain themselves either lucidly or persuasively. On the contrary, there are strong signs that some artistic clans find clarity, like cleanliness and tidiness, reactionary and repulsive. Order is bad, analysis is bourgeois and inhuman, the heart is always superior to the head. Yet the old basic fears of being misunderstood and unloved remain, even among those who make the greatest efforts to achieve these states, and one therefore finds 'explanation' and 'communication' being attempted in non-verbal ways. The result, not surprisingly, is that all that is ultimately achieved is the exchange of verbal jargon for a non-verbal kind.

The antics of the Anglo-American group of Conceptual artists known as Art and Language illustrates the point. In 1969, after much argument and soul-searching, the group came to the provisional conclusion that the most suitable medium of what it referred to as the 'language' of art was words. It therefore began to publish a journal. This soon came to be regarded as an error of judgement, a step backwards. The journal was given up and replaced with a series of messages to the world on tape, microfilm and posters. To begin with, the members of the group used a version of the methods of British analytical philosophy, but later they pillaged a wide range of philosophical, scientific and sociological disciplines and vocabularies in a never-ending search for the tools with which they could think and express themselves. Their usual method was to present the world with a collage of what they had found in the writings and sayings of other seekers after truth. The resulting wilfully crazy assembly of words was almost incomprehensible. Whatever it may have meant to those within the group – and we have no evidence that it did, in fact, mean anything – it was totally baffling to anyone outside it; jargon in its oldest and purest form, the twittering of birds.

Earlier in this chapter, it was suggested that the cultivated appreciation of food and wine has a right to be considered one of the arts. It is certainly an art, with a rich jargon of its own, more particularly on the wine side. Wines are uncomplicated, easy to drink, fuller and more fleshy and possess great depth and colour. They achieve an attractive balance, are eminently sound and potable, have an attractive bone structure, slump into early flabbiness, have no inhibitions, and show great depth and finesse. Asked to define these strange terms, a wine merchant or wine writer is likely to reply that they cannot be defined but that everyone in the business knows what they mean, an answer which may be true but remains unsatisfactory. It is one thing for two wine merchants in earnest professional converse to discuss a wine's soundness, depth and bone structure, but quite another matter to use such terms in a catalogue or newspaper article aimed at the public. On the first kind of occasion, the jargon may well function as a secret language between brothers and colleagues, but on the second it merely, and one fears deliberately, mystifies. Yet this sort of thing is very common:

> The Ayala, however, is one of the most beautiful champagnes I have ever tasted – the lightly fresh bouquet reminding me of a herbaceous border after rain, emerges and develops from the bottle like the genie in the fairy-stories and continues to delight the drinker throughout. The taste combines fullness with absolute dryness, so that as the wine passes from the palate, there is left an impression of supreme nobility.[48]

The herbaceous border simile is innocent enough and causes no problem, but the 'impression of supreme nobility' conveys remarkably little to at least one reader. It is club language, secret society language, or, as one writer has astutely termed it, the language of wine-buffs. There is a possibility that beer may be moving closer to having a jargon of its own. As a shrewd and knowledgeable observer of the situation has recently put it,

> There is clearly one area which beer connoisseurs will have to cultivate in order to approach in influence of wine-buffs – the language of appreciation. The experienced beer-drinker does not seem to get beyond 'thin but hoppy', 'dark and nutty', and the occasional 'smooth and malty'. Boston quotes Hardy's description of the beer of Casterbridge in *The Trumpet Major* . . . 'brisk as a volcano; piquant, yet without a twang; luminous as an autumn sunset'.[49]

No sensible person would wish to discourage the habit of using words in an adventurous or poetic fashion. Anything which adds life and vigour to the mother tongue is welcome. But there are fields in which snobbery encourages the growth of jargon that is not particularly lively or richly-coloured and that serves only to encourage those who prize any badge which marks them off from the herd and who value words for their ability to achieve this. The ultimate food jargon in the English-speaking world is the kind of French that gives menus a flavour more distinguished than the food they describe. The wine-writers, on the other hand, exercise their skill by means of English, hoping that their status will be considerably improved by heavy use of the jargon that goes with the business.

When that great populariser of the pleasures of the table, André Simon, was once being admiringly discussed by Charles Morgan, the ridiculous aspect of some of the great wine-fancier's language was suggested. In Morgan's words:

> What you say of wines is so dangerously often applicable to ladies that it may cause confusion in the minds of our younger members. Take this for example: 'Somewhat short in the nose, she gave more than she promised – a good fault. Full of life: silky, serious, robust and elusive; refined and expanding; she left behind, as she departed, a sense of complete gratification without the least feeling of satiety.' Really, *what* are you describing? Château Ausone 1902 or Cleopatra?[50]

To this, the only truthful reply would have been, 'I make no clear distinction between ladies and wine. Both deserve to be admired and cherished.' Morgan, however, was writing before the wine experts began to show what they could really do with English.

The food writers and menu composers have produced a special jargon of their own, calculated to grade up every dish on offer. The words are very frequently far more appetising than the food they purport to describe. A favourite trick is the unnecessary adjective: 'Small pieces of tender pork cooked with onion, white wine, capsicums and cream.'[51] This may be encouraging to the visitor who has arrived at the restaurant expecting to find tough, stringy pork, but, to those who are accustomed to dining in places where the meat is eatable, 'tender' may well seem redundant unless, on the pattern of 'garden peas', 'tender pork' is now to be regarded as a compound noun.

The Americans are much given to the prose-poem type of menu. We have an abundance of such delicacies as 'Vanilla Ice Cream floating in a frosty goblet of old-fashioned root beer, topped with a blanket of whipped cream, chopped nuts and a cherry',[52] where the ration of emotive words, 'floating', 'frosty', 'old-fashioned', 'goblet', 'blanket' is extremely high. The bare statement, 'Vanilla Ice Cream in root beer, topped with whipped cream, chopped nuts and a cherry' is evidently felt to contain insufficient appeal. The thought of ice-cream in root beer is not altogether pleasant to anyone who has been fortunate enough to retain a palate.

North America and its satellites have come to accept their foodmongers' jargon as part of the order of things. So we have 'Four heaping scoops of vanilla ice cream, ladled over with hot fudge.'[53] and 'A snow-white mountain of cottage cheese, with center filled with fresh fruit sections.'[54] Butter is not just butter, but 'creamery butter'[55] and one of the most ordinary and tasteless cheeses in the world, imported Dutch Edam, becomes 'tangy, firm, rewarding'.[56] The hyphenated adjective is considered to be of great importance in making the food appear more interesting than it really is. Fish is consequently no longer fried in butter, but 'butter-fried, garnished with soft roe, lemon and tomato'.[57]

Food-jargon is international now, and it sometimes passes beyond absurdity and exaggeration and into sheer nonsense. Twenty or thirty years ago, when fish was upgraded to seafood, it was still understood that one was eating creatures which had once lived in the sea. Over-use has now apparently removed all meaning from this particular piece of jargon, and it has become possible to refer to 'the Cameo Restaurant, which specialises in maritime seafoods'.[58]

In the great days of French cooking, when the preparation and serving of food and drink was brought as close to an art-form as it is ever likely to be, the phrase 'haute cuisine' had a real meaning. Nowadays it is mere jargon, used as a synonym and a euphemism for 'expensive'. Nobody should be deluded by such idiocies as: 'Superb haute cuisine menu, designed to meet the demands of the discerning businessman'[59] or 'The à la carte menu lists a delicious selection of haute cuisine dishes, all served with a panache that only the finest cuisine can offer.'[60] Language like this is aimed at snobs who have never known the real thing. It is jargon at its most immoral.

4 The Near-Professions

The dividing line between the near-professions, the subject of this chapter, and the would-be professions, which are considered in Chapter Five, must be, to some extent, a matter of opinion and prejudice. For practical purposes, a near-profession is one which seems likely to achieve full status before the end of the present century and a would-be profession is one in which the aspirations of its members seem unlikely to be realised in the foreseeable future. The principal examples of the first category are taken to be teaching, psychology, philosophy and sociology, and of the second, advertising, journalism, economics and management. It is worth recording at this point that all eight of these trades, vocations or occupations are among the leading jargon producers of our time, and all for the same reason; they are trying desperately hard to be recognised as a branch of science, knowing in their hearts that this is something they can never become. They long to play in the same league as the physicists, chemists, biologists and metallurgists and to have a professional language comparable to:

> Aluminium is the most important alloying addition to magnesium, and it is added in quantities up to about 11 per cent. As with most other alloys, the magnesium alloys may be classified into those which are cast and those which are wrought. The casting alloys are of two types. The first contains magnesium with 2 per cent of manganese and the second type contains 8 to 10 per cent aluminium with 0.5 per cent zinc and 0.25 per cent manganese. The latter alloys in particular possess good mechanical properties, which may be further improved by heat-treatment.[1]

In their efforts to create a special language for themselves, the near-professions frequently put themselves in the unenviable position of being found funny. It is surely a healthy sign that, for all the prestige and power of science, we are still able to laugh at such ridiculous striving after 'precision' as 'Their libidinal impulses being reciprocated they activated their individual erotic drives and interpreted them within the same frame of reference',[2] when all that is meant is the old-fashioned, 'They fell in love and got married'. When we laugh equally heartily at all attempts to push scientific and technical language outside their proper boundaries, we shall be well on the road to linguistic salvation. A large part of contemporary jargon could be tamed, if not abolished, if only it were subjected to sufficiently heavy and frequent bursts of ridicule. It survives and multiplies by being respected, ignored or attacked head on.

If one considers, perhaps generously, that sociology is destined to become a fully-fledged profession one day, it is useful to consider how it expresses itself at present since, in the opinion of many observers of our contemporary world, sociologists generate more jargon in the course of a year than any other body of educated people. How far is such a view justified, bearing in mind that the sociologist, like any other academic, works by trying to impose a pattern on a mass of material which, in its raw state, contains little order? In attempting to discover acceptable models by which human activity can be studied and interpreted, he faces a peculiarly difficult task. It is hardly surprising that he should attempt to carry it out with the help of a special language and that such a language should constitute an important part of his discipline. Two questions have to be asked, however: does all sociological language have a beneficial effect, and are some at least of the terms a sociologist uses no more than bricks in a protective wall which he builds around himself?

Consider this passage, taken from an American analysis of the journeys undertaken by people who live and work in cities.

> In order to examine the composition of journeys and the association among trip purposes, we need to simulate actual journeys over a typical day. The key to simulating journeys is the coefficient of linkage of trips from one purpose or activity to another. The linkage coefficient is simply the ratio of person trips from an origin purpose to some destination trip purpose to the total trips from the origin purpose. In a matrix table like the above the linkage coefficient of any cell is found by dividing the person trips in that cell by the sum of the row in which it lies. The ratio is expressed as
>
> $$LC_{ij} = \frac{X_{ij}}{\sum^{n}_{k=1} X_{ik}}$$
>
> where X_{ij} = trips from purpose i to purpose j
>
> $\sum^{n}_{k=1} X_{ik}$ = all trips from purpose i

> The matrix of linkage coefficients is a stochastic matrix where each row sums to one. And the linkage coefficient can be interpreted as a measure of the probability of a trip from a given activity being destined to a particular activity.
>
> To calculate an estimate of the number and type of multiple trip journeys we treat our matrix of linkage coefficients as an absorbing Markov chain. Markov chains consist of states and steps, or transitions, between states. The Markov chain process has been aptly described in terms of a frog jumping from one to another of a group of lily pads. Each of the lily pads can be considered a state, and the steps are the frog's jumps from one lily pad to another. The probability that the frog will land on any of the pads when jumping from the lily pad he currently occupies is described by transition probabilities. These probabilities depend only on which lily pad he is occupying before he makes the jump.
>
> The frog moving from one lily pad to another is comparable to the urban resident journeying from one activity to another.[3]

The author of this book has chosen to study an exceptionally chaotic aspect of human activity, the daily movements of tens of thousands of people in the course of earning a living, keeping alive and amusing themselves. In order to do this, to distinguish and describe a pattern, he decides to use a language which, to many of those who are not professionally involved, may well appear to be jargon – 'trip purposes', 'person trips', 'destination trip purpose', and so on. Only when he has done this – and the process of classification necessarily simplifies and therefore distorts the reasons why people are moving about – can he begin to apply his second stage of discipline, the statistical analysis of journeys. This involves the use of specialised mathematical terms, such as 'linkage coefficients', 'Markov chains' and 'stochastic matrix', which set the sociologist further and further apart from his fellow citizens, part of whose life he is studying. He is doomed or, if one prefers, predestined to professional language, if not to jargon. Yet, for some reason which is worth exploring, one does not resent his language or feel that it is bogus or pretentious in the way that one does a piece of sociological flag-waving of this type:

> If the objective self-identity as the behavioural and evaluative expectations which the person anticipates others having about himself is significant for the communicated self-identity, regardless of its source the former may be regarded as a referent other.[4]

This sentence is utter jargon and nonsense from beginning to end, and both its author and the editor of the *British Journal of Sociology* should be thoroughly ashamed of themselves for foisting it on those who take an interest in sociology. One feels not so much puzzled by it as cheated and angry. Nobody should write so badly and expect to get away with it, but the presence of such an article in a learned journal is evidence, not only that the author has got away with it, but that he has received the accolade of his peers at the same time. If it is necessary to express oneself in this way in order to be acknowledged as a sociologist of repute, one feels, then it would be better for mankind if sociology dropped its professional claims forthwith.

This, of course, would be unfair, because there are a few sociologists at least who are repelled by such jargon and who see no reason to make use of it. But they represent, one fears, a very small minority. On both sides of the Atlantic, in books, articles and reviews, one is likely to come across this: 'March's major hypothesis was that the range within which a group can manipulate the orientations of its members increases monotonically with an increase in the group's autonomy'[5]; or, with an even greater determination not to sound like other men, this: 'Status endogamy at the highest level. Here, Sahlins' proposition is weakened insofar as there is more hypergamy and hypogamy at the élite level in the most differentiated societies than in societies of intermediate differentiation.'[6]

In case there should be the occasional sociologist who is not immediately aware of the meaning of hypergamy and hypogamy, an explanatory footnote is provided. Hypergamy, it appears, is 'Marriage of the female into a higher social stratum' and hypogamy 'Marriage of the female into a lower social stratum'. 'This', the author believes, 'suggests that the greater rate of vertical occupational mobility in American society is due almost wholly to sheer quantitative occupational demand differences rather than to universalistic achievement values and norms.'

It may be, however, that we have here, too, a sentence whose meaning may not be crystal-clear to everyone who picks up the book. Jargon, in fact, has been defined in terms of more jargon, which is a curious way of going about the business.

One should distinguish, however, between jargon and sheer ignorance of the meaning of words. There are semi-literate sociologists, just as there are semi-literate engineers, artists or doctors, but with sociology it is especially difficult to distinguish between an author whose command of language is inadequate and one who is using an ordinary word which has been taken into the sociological vocabulary in a particular technical sense. Consider, for instance, this extract from an article in *Sociology*: 'With language as a cultural product embodying the typifications sedimented in the history of the society.'[7] In the English used by people who are not sociologists, 'sediment' is solid matter which sinks to the bottom of a liquid. It is not the happiest metaphor for a society's cultural survivals, suggesting as it does a kind of mud or silt, rather than the most lasting and significant creations of our ancestors. Did the writer mean 'embedded' or 'enshrined'? Does 'sediment' have a different meaning for sociologists and, if so, why? Or was this particular person simply ill-informed or careless? The third possibility seems the most likely.

The following passage is solid jargon:

> The examples given suggest that the multiformity of environmental apprehension and the exclusivity of abstract semantic conceptions constitute a crucial distinction. Semantic responses to qualities, environmental or other, tend to abstract each individual quality as though it were to be experienced in isolation, with nothing else impinging. But in actual environmental experience, our judgements of attributes are constantly affected by the entire milieu, and the connectivities such observations suggest reveal this multiform complexity. Semantic response is generally a consequence of reductive categorization, environmental response or synthesizing holism.'[8]

The jargon here is inexcusable, because, hidden underneath it there is a train of thought which can be expressed much more simply. 'The multiformity of environmental apprehension', for instance, means that we are aware of our environment in a number of different ways. 'Semantic responses' are the words we use to describe what we see and 'environmental experience' is our observation of our surroundings. The final sentence is so pretentious and absurd that, as a penance, the authors should be locked up without food or water until they can produce an acceptable translation.

So, too, should the person responsible for the following academic masterpiece, in which all that is in fact being said is that it is more effective to punish a naughty child while he is actually in the act of being naughty, instead of waiting until afterwards.

> A factor of considerable importance in naturalistic socialization contexts is the timing of punishment. In home situations, punishment is often delayed beyond the completion of the deviant behaviour. Does the timing of the administration of a punisher affect its effectiveness as a means of inhibiting undesirable behaviour? Mowrer (1960) has provided a theoretical framework for predicting the effects of the timing of punishment. According to Mowrer, each component of a response sequence provides sensory feedback in the form of response-produced kinesthetic and proprioceptive cues. Punishment may be administered at any point during the sequence of responses and result in a relatively direct association of a fear-motivated avoidance response with the response-produced cues occurring at the temporal locus of punishment. If the punishment is administered at the initiation of the deviant response sequence, the maximal degree of fear is attached to the cues produced by the instrumental acts involved in initiating the sequence. In this case,

> subsequent initiation of the sequence will arouse anxiety that activates incompatible avoidance responses, which are reinforced by anxiety reduction if they are sufficiently strong to forestall the deviant behaviour.[9]

Which many parents have discovered already, in self-defence and without the benefit of theory or the realisation that a child who cries when it is smacked is providing sensory feedback.

Yet many, if not most sociologists would like to be regarded as practical, useful people, analysing society for its own good, helping the world to move on to another and, one hopes, better stage of development. The sad thing is that they find it so difficult to say this plainly. Some strange demon compels them to wrap their faith up in so many layers of brown words that great patience is required from anyone who sets out to unwrap the parcel. Here is such a parcel:

> Rooted in a limited personal reality, resonating some sentiments but not others, and embedded in certain domain assumptions, every social theory facilitates the pursuit of some but not of all courses of *action*, and thus encourages us to change or to accept the world as it is, to say yea or nay to it. In a way, every theory is a discreet obituary or celebration for some social system.
>
> The sentiments resonated by a social theory provide an immediate but privatized mood, an experience that inhibits or fosters anticipated courses of public and political conduct, and thus may exacerbate or resolve internal uncertainties or conflicts about the possibilities or successful outcomes. Similarly, domain assumptions entail beliefs about what is real in the world and thus have implications about what it is possible to *do*, to *change* in the world; the values they entail indicate what courses of action are desirable and thus shape conduct. In this sense, every theory and every theorist idealogizes social reality.[10]

'Domain assumptions', 'discreet obituary', 'privatized mood', 'resonated' – the insistence that the social scientist is not as other men is frantic and never-ending. Without their jargon to sustain them, such people would, one feels, wither away and die. They are, one might almost say, jargon made man. The sociologist is, however, quick to insist that the subject of his study, the reason for his existence, is not man but society, and that words which might indeed be described as jargon if they referred to ordinary human activites are not jargon if they are used to observe and assess a social process, since, with no traditional language of their own, sociologists have had to take their words where they can find them and adapt to their own needs. As one American has put it:

> It makes a substantial difference whether one views the autonomy or

> alienation of social structures from people as a normal condition to be accepted or as an endemic and recurrent disease to be opposed. It is inherent in the very occupational ideology of many modern sociologists, faced as they are with the professional task of distinguishing their own from competing academic disciplines, not only to stress the potency and autonomy of social structures – and therefore the dependence of persons – but also to accept this as normal, rather than asking: Under what conditions does it occur? Are there not differences in the degree to which social structures get out of hand and live independently of their members? What accounts for these differences?[11]

It is significant that this author refers to the sociologists' 'professional task of distinguishing their own from competing academic disciplines'. One way of doing this is to make clear that their prime concern is with social structures, rather than with individual behaviour. Even so, it seems a little exaggerated to speak of this as an 'occupational ideology'. A body of ideas, perhaps, but hardly an 'ideology', which suggests a driving force, a theory which provides the motivation for a person's life and activity, the theological basis of Christianity, Communism, Zionism or the Palestine Liberation Movement. The sociologist who chooses to speak of his 'occupational ideology' is giving the accepted sense of the word a perverse twist to suit his immediate purpose.

Any expert or specialist will tend to view natural phenomena or human circumstances from his own particular point of view. He will select, describe and analyse those features which strike him as significant, within the limits of the discipline which conditions his thinking. We are told:

> More specifically a high science methodology tends to distil the complexity of social situations into a search for the effects of a few highly formalized and specially defined 'variables', whose presence often cannot be gauged by direct inspection but requires special instruments employed under special conditions. Thus the 'variables' sociologists study often do not exist for laymen; they are not what laymen see when they look about themselves. High science methodologies, in effect, create a gap between what the sociologist as sociologist deals with and what he (like others) confronts as an ordinary person, experiencing his *own* existence. Thus even when he undertakes studies in the sociology of knowledge, exploring, say, the effects of 'class position', 'reference groups', or 'income levels' on intellectual activities, it is easy for him to feel that he is talking about someone else, perhaps some other sociologist, not about himself and his own life.[12]

This gap between society as seen through the eyes of the sociologist and society as it appears to the layman, is created and widened by the tools the sociologist uses, by his technical vocabulary. Whether one calls it a language barrier or a jargon barrier is immaterial. It exists, and the fact of its existence inevitably breeds suspicion and even hatred among non-sociologists, who feel that 'their' words are being grossly and wilfully mishandled and corrupted. The social scientist himself has to live in two worlds. On the other hand, he has a mother-tongue in which he has to make himself intelligible, like anyone else who belongs to his language group, and on the other he is required to show himself skilful at handling his occupational language. This may, on occasion, involve walking a verbal tightrope, since the same words often form part of his two vocabularies.

Sociology is in the same position as any other theoretical discipline. It has to have a terminology, a language which is precise and which permits unambiguous communication between initiates.[13] Given this clear and exact terminology, theories can be formulated and published, research can be carried out and information analysed. However incomprehensible such writing may be to the public at large, it provides a common basis of understanding, a code, which can be shared by others working in the same and related fields. Without precise, agreed terms, theories cannot be worked out, research loses itself in a maze of ambiguity and communication among members of what is claimed to be a profession degenerates into intellectual chaos, as a game of chess or football inevitably would, if the rules were not laid down in advance.

It is particularly necessary that sociology should develop a precise language, if it is to become a discipline – some people doubt the possibility – because its subject matter, man and society, is one with which everyone is familiar, or can claim to be. The ways in which people rear and educate their children, the subtleties of rank and status, the interlocking networks of power and influence – all these are experienced, if not understood, by everyone who lives within a particular culture. For this reason, nobody can remain detached from the material the sociologist studies. In everyday speech, such features of our lives are discussed and thought about in a highly emotive way. The terms used by the man in the street to express his thinking on such topics are value-laden to an extent which no sociologist could tolerate, if he is to hope for any respect within academic circles. He must therefore circumscribe and narrow their meaning if they are to be of any use to him and to those who are not sociologists such an action may seem arrogant or pharasaical. At these moments, the person in question is likely to be accused of using jargon. It is a calculated risk.

'When we transfer terms like "personality" or "law" or "cause" from everyday language into scientific usage, we must always make decisions for which we ourselves take the responsibility. We give up certain connotations which these terms have in order to make the remainder more precise and more easily amenable to verification and proof.'[14] This is to present sociological language in the most favourable way. There is, regrettably, another possibility, which we have stated earlier in a different context. The writer or speaker may, in fact, have little or nothing to say. He has learnt the technical language and he has acquired a facility for adding one element to another, as if he were stringing a row of beads. What he produces, however, is a sham, a fraud, looking impressive but expressing nothing of any real value. He has observed the verbal ritual and so justified his membership of the club. He is to that extent respectable and it is unlikely that his fellow sociologists will denounce him as a charlatan, any more than an incompetent doctor will be exposed by his colleagues. Who, then, is to strip the veil from him and show him as he is? It can, in practice, be carried out only by an outside operator acting on behalf of the community, a kind of linguistic ombudsman. He would, one hopes, be equipped with some form of electronic rubbish-cum-jargon detector, to give credibility to his decisions and to absolve him of all taint of prejudice.

One passes easily and naturally from the sociologists to the philosophers, who have somewhat similar problems, in that both see their task to be the observation of patterns and principle in very pedestrian material and both are given to using ordinary words in extraordinary ways. Both are frequently accused of indulging in jargon, but there is an important difference between the attitude of the public towards the two. The sociologist is likely to be seen as a person who uses words as a smoke-screen, the philosopher as someone who makes a great deal of fuss about nothing, a pernickety fellow who like a lawyer, refuses to take anything for granted and who crosses all his ts not once, but three times.

A philosopher, unlike a sociologist, is very likely to state his problem in the simplest and clearest of terms and to move into progressively more professional and 'difficult' language as he goes along. Here is an example, from a book by Richard Swinburne, the present Professor of Philosophy at the University of Keele. The layman has no difficulty whatever at the beginning.

> A large number of ravens are observed, and found to be black, the same colour as present MA gowns of the University of Oxford, the oldest university of the English speaking world. Two hypotheses are proposed:
> h_1 : all ravens are black
> h_2 : all ravens are the same colour as Oxma gowns[15]

An 'Oxma gown' is obligingly defined as 'an MA gown of the oldest university in the English speaking world' and the author then proceeds to develop his argument in terms which some will find attractive and some infuriating.

> h_1 and h_2 are equally accurate in their predictions so far $P(e/h_1.k)$ =

> $P(e/h_2.k)$, but they make conflicting predictions about what will be the colour of ravens if the colour of Oxford MA gowns is changed. On the evidence h_1 is more probable than h_2 because h_1 is simpler than h_2. Why is h_1 simpler? Because '*B*', 'black', is a more natural predicate, describes a property which in our conceptual scheme is a property more essential to ravens than '*C*', 'has the same colour as Oxma gowns'. ('*B*' and '*C*' are epistemologically independent; one can find out whether an object has the same colour as an Oxma gown by comparing them together without comparing them with standard objects to find out for certain what the colour is, and conversely.) We cannot avoid the force of the argument in this and similar examples by claiming that in actual fact we have a lot of evidence (*e*) to show that 'black' is a more constant property of birds than 'of the same colour as Oxma gowns'(*H*), because, even if we do, as we saw on pp. 106f. it is only in virtue of the considerations which we have been discussing (viz. considerations of relative simplicity) that *e* gives any probability to H.[16]

The non-expert reader may be puzzled by the mathematical formula in the second line, he may need to look up 'epistemologically' in a dictionary, and he may find the contact with a philosophical mind strange. But close-reasoning and mathematics do not, by themselves, constitute jargon. This is a good piece of professional writing and requires no other justification or defence. Nor does another passage in the same book, which is likely to be wholly unintelligible to the layman:

> There is a number of kinds of sets of infinite numbers of nomological propositions to each of which we must attribute zero intrinsic probability. In the first place we must attribute zero intrinsic probability to any hypotheses of the form '$Pr(Q/A) = p$', with the possible exception of '$Pr(Q/A) = 1$' and '$Pr(Q/A) = 0$' (and by similar arguments to any hypotheses of the form 'π $(Q/A = 0$'). As we saw in Chapter 11 p can take any value among the infinite number of values in the real number continuum between 0 and 1. That we must attribute to each such hypothesis zero intrinsic probability can be seen with the aid of Principle A (see p.43). In it let e be our total evidence and k be a tautology. Then we can imagine an infinite number of situations in which any one such hypothesis h_1 is as accurate in its predictions as a different such hypothesis h_n.[17]

There is no other way in which the author could say what he had to say. He is in full communication with anyone who has troubled to learn the language, just as one morse code operator can understand another without difficulty. So long as a philosopher is content to make contact only with his equals, the fact that he is using a private language is unobjectionable. But the moment he steps outside that circle, which modern philosophers rarely do, he has a duty to find a way of expressing himself intelligibly to a wider audience. If he attempts to blind that wider audience with jargon, he is vulnerable to attack.

One of the saddest features of contemporary society is that professional philosophers have so little to say to ordinary people. The hungry sheep look up and are fed, not by philosophers, but by psychologists, sociologists and politicians. Possibly for this reason, the philosophers are not greatly given to jargon. They exist in a small closed world, which the general public is not encouraged to penetrate. They feel little need to strike attitudes or to impress humanity at large. It might perhaps be better if they did.

The public demands the priestly services of psychologists, sociologists and perhaps of political theorists, but it feels in no particular need of help from philosophers. Once a demand exists, there will always be people to meet it, and, as the advertisers know very well, people like to feel that they are getting value for money when they make their purchases. An effective way of giving satisfaction is to dress the goods up in fine-sounding language, which psychologists in particular can do with considerable skill.

This is particularly true of educational psychologists, who are, second only to those concerned with business management, the most prolific generators of jargon in the Western world. There are no richer jargon mines than the *Journal of Educational Psychology* and the *Journal of Educational Research.* A small selection of extracts from these publications will make the point.

> Research on cue utilisation in person perception suggests that person judgements may be as much a function of the rater's personalised notions of tract interrelationships as they are a function of the available clues.[18]

> The role of reinforcement as a causative agent in increasing the probability of future recurrence of particular responses is examined experimentally and subjected to statistical scrutiny. The reinforcement's immediacy to the response and the subject's awareness of it are found to elicit the desired response by means other than situational chance thereby indicating its potential usefulness for guiding behavior into desirable channels.[19]

> Analysis of covariance partialling out the pre-test achievement on the physiology test was used to adjust the means and the within sums of squares prior to the use of Dunn's 'c' procedure.[20]

> Scale R (favorable versus unfavorable attitudes toward democratic class-

room procedures) has a substantial negative loading on the factor indicating that subjects having a high score on measures of analytic set tended to possess unfavourable attitudes in this regard.[21]

Darley and Hagenah point to prestige drives among youth as an important source of occupational choice-vocational interest congruency.[22]

The ability to simulate the lexical statistics of a particular word swarm is probably quite adaptive in school situations.[23]

How can an educated person bring himself to write such dreadful stuff? To this there are two possible answers. The first is that he is not an educated person, but a highly paid, highly trained performing monkey. He has not read widely, he does not have a cultivated taste in literature, art or any other civilised, mind-broadening pursuit. When he is not practising some form of educational psychology, he is tinkering with his car, mowing his lawn or watching football on television. He has certain skills, but no taste, no feeling for elegance. His life-style is, not to mince words, low.

The second and more charitable possibility is that he is bi-lingual, speaking and writing English agreeably away from his work and producing monstrous sentences like those quoted above when he is at his desk or in front of a lecture audience. In this case, he rarely, if ever, has the two kinds of English in the same focus. They do not influence one another in any way and he is content that it should be so.

Neither of these explanations is wholly satisfactory, as one can easily show by means of a simple test. Ask half-a-dozen educational theorists or psychologists, separately and individually, to read the six short extracts given above and then, with the words fresh in their minds, to say, in their own words what each means. The exercise may or may not be popular, but it will effectively dispel any idea that language such as this makes for rapid, easy, foolproof communication between one expert and another. It does nothing of the kind. If, then, 'an important source of occupational choice-vocational interest congruency' makes the professional's mind work as hard as the layman's, if some meaning is to be squeezed out of such ugly jargon, why does the writer express himself this way, instead of saying 'an important source of congruency between occupational choice and vocational interest', which allows the reader to work things out in logical stages? Why go for the compressed, unnatural form, which the human brain cannot handle, instead of something more expanded and more logical? The answer, apart from sheer ignorance and clumsiness, can only be an ever-present impulse to prove that one is not as other men. If the outside world uses prepositions, the expert must leave them out. Two nouns glued together – 'cue utilisation', 'person perception', 'tract interrelationships', 'word swarm' – are proof of academic quality.

Masters of this assembly-line language can use it to create a rhythm which sends the reader into a trance and which, unless he fights its hypnotic influence very hard, can anaesthetise his critical faculty. The long chains of polysyllables have the effect of a drug, which causes one to become oblivious of the fact that what one is reading is meaningless. Anyone who doubts this should sit quietly in a comfortable chair, in a pleasantly warm room, and ask a friend with a soothing voice to read the following passages aloud, over and over like a series of Tibetan prayers. Within fifteen minutes one will be either peacefully asleep or in a state of waking bliss.

> Rohwer has treated methods of presentation as external analogues of hypothetical internal mental activities engaged in by persons who are efficient learners. The notion is advanced that successful paired-associate learning is promoted by the elaboration of the raw elements to be acquired so as to invest them with membership in a single semantic set, either by lodging them in the same linguistic unit, as in a sentence, or in the same pictorial unit, as in an action episode.[24]

> Smedslund proposed that a state of cognitive conflict was the precursor of the cognitive reorganization that was required to support conservation. The proposal is consonant with the Piagetian notion that problems provoke cognitive disequilibrium, the resolution of which requires a new integration of distinct operations, such as simultaneously, instead of separately, attending to height and width in substance conservation or both end points in length conservation.[25]

> The second aim of the studies also followed from the partitioning of the independent variable: to assess, through the regression coefficients, the actual contribution of each of the prior disposition estimates to the overall rating of initial confidence.[26]

> Factor 3 is a 'hostile-negativistic' pattern, with its very high loading on negative reinforcement, related to a good deal of questioning and with very high negative loadings on several of the more sympathetic interpersonal qualities.[27]

Language like this is anodyne. Far from having a mentally bracing effect and making one concentrate, it paralyses the brain. Not only is one unable to devote one's energies to it, in order to extract whatever meaning it may contain; one has no desire to do so.

It is important to notice that the worst psychological jargon, especially in the educational field, is to be found not in books, but in articles in learned journals, which are the places where academic reputations are made. Before a paper is accepted for publication in such a journal, it has to be read and approved by one or more referees, who assess its 'quality' and either rubber-stamp it or reject it, possibly with suggestions as to how it might be improved and eventually made suitable. The appearance of the paper in print therefore certifies that what the author has written has been found acceptable by his peers, a fact which is important to him in his career. But it also means that the jargon to which we have drawn attention has passed the professional test. It is not only jargon, but officially approved jargon, which, to an outside observer, is even more discouraging. Those in positions of power and influence have seen nothing wrong with such sentences as 'A set is a cognitive process activated by a stimulus or stimuli perceived by a person in environmental situations, determining how one is predisposed to respond to what is intended to in a given situation',[28] and have given them their imprimatur. Under such conditions, the disease is bound to spread. If readers of the Journal see what is printed already, they are bound to conclude that one must write in this way in order to get one's work published. Sloppy or non-existent editing inevitably produces sloppy authors. No wideawake editor, sensitive to the meaning of words, could have allowed this sentence past his scrutiny: 'Although girls tended to make slightly higher scores than boys on the reproduction and transposition tasks, the differences were unreliable.'[29] In their anxiety to remove all value-judgements from their professional language, writers and speakers on education take great pains to avoid such old-fashioned and emotive words as 'lazy', 'idle', 'stupid', 'clever' or 'poor'. They refer instead to 'disadvantaged home environments', 'educationally and socially advantaged groups', 'higher-aptitude students', 'less-deprived homes', 'underprivileged children', 'high verbal-ability subjects', and so on. It is not clear whom these euphemisms – for that is what in fact they are – can be supposed to benefit. They may well prove to be a hindrance to clear thinking and effective action. So long as there were good homes and poor homes, feckless mothers and hard-working, responsible mothers, intelligent children and dim children, one knew where one was. But the 'underprivileged boy' is underprivileged by comparison with whom? What is the norm? Is it the 'privileged boy', the 'average-privileged boy', or what? There have always been children who are good at writing and speaking the English language and who could spell properly, and others who had very little skill in such matters. Why is it reckoned to be better or more helpful to talk of 'high verbal-ability subjects'? Who functions better as a result?

The answer is, nobody, but one can easily see why this new educational vocabulary became inevitable and why it is so widely used. Two distinct trends combined to make it popular. The first was a belief, amounting to an article of faith, among 'progressive educationists' – that clever children, especially those from middle-class homes, had had things their own way for far too long and that the time had come to show more concern for 'ordinary' or 'average' boys and girls. This meant, in effect, creating an education system which was geared to the weak, rather than the strong, a development which coincided with similar thinking in the political field. Everything had to be done, therefore, to prevent 'ordinary' children from feeling in any way inferior to bright children, and a major weapon in the campaign was the creation of a new vocabulary, which would soften and obscure the differences between the fortunate and the unfortunate. The sharp edges were to be removed from society.

At the same time, during the 1950s and 1960s, the social sciences were beginning to make their presence felt. They were forming their own language, and they found no difficulty in giving their blessing to the kind of phrases the progressive education movement was discovering for itself. The two sets of needs fused and the resulting disadvantaged-home-environment swept nearly everything before it. The conventions that have become established in this way have grown deep roots and it is going to be extremely difficult to change them or get rid of them, although the need for them no longer exists to the extent that it did twenty years ago.[30]

Educational theorists, like any other body of people engaged in academic writing and research, have a living and a respect to earn. They are unlikely to achieve this by being either brief or simple. It is much more probable that they will build up a reputation for themselves by finding new and complicated ways of investigating and analysing familiar forms of behaviour and by presenting their findings in language which proves that they understand and observe the rules appropriate to their calling. They will always, for example, speak of 'teacher behaviour', rather than 'the behaviour of teachers', 'teacher satisfaction', instead of 'satisfaction among teachers', and 'teacher effectiveness', not 'the effectiveness of teachers'. They will home in on expressions like 'stimuli-response habit-hierarchies', and 'reading readiness scores', and show great fondness for 'appropriate verbal mediators', 'bidimensional solutions', and 'uncrystallised cognitive or reward structures'.

If articles appear to contain more of this kind of jargon than books, it is only because the author of a book, with no referees to satisfy, can afford to ease up a little now and then and does not have quite the same need to stun his readers into acquiescence. He has two or three hundred pages with which to obtain his effects, and can dilute the jargon a little.

Here, for example, is an American book on the effectiveness of different teaching styles. In order to get the study under way, it was necessary to split a teaching technique into what appeared to be its component parts. Then, 'In order to identify the underlying dimensions of teacher behavior, these variables were factor-analysed, using the principle factors method. Ten factors were extracted, accounting for 73 per cent of the variance. These were rotated to orthogonal simple structure by the varimax method.'[31] This is all properly quantitative and professional, and it may just possibly lead to a better understanding of what makes a good teacher, although a teacher, it could be suggested, is something more than the sum of his behaviour-factors.

We are then faced with a difficulty which arises directly from the jargon the author chooses to employ. It occurs at the beginning of this paragraph: 'Effective teacher communication may be satisfying to students for a number of reasons. It may help provide the student with a sense of cognitive completeness and control; it may help him feel intellectually secure (because able to understand), in a sense, validated in his academic confidence.'[32] Does 'teacher communication' mean 'communication with a teacher', or 'communication by a teacher'? Since this is the whole point of the passage, it is well to know which is intended, but if the writer is so professionally inhibited from using prepositions, those unworthy hallmarks of the conversational style, we can only guess, in the knowledge that there is a fifty-fifty chance that we shall be wrong.

This book shows, in a most interesting way, how easy it is for social scientists to live in two worlds, without apparently being aware of the fact. On the one hand, they can use the jargon, the language of their professional world, almost instinctively:

> Perhaps the culturally developed tolerance of females for the passive role of a listener allows them to function more effectively in a lecture situation, particularly when the instructor is a male .... Lecturing may be seen as the appropriate masculine teacher role by females.[33]

> Cultural-value similarity may be most relevant to the kind of learning which takes place in psychotherapy, while the shared technical vocabulary would be most relevant to setting a framework for efficient transmission of information.[34]

and, in the same book, they can record that:

> . . . each criminal specialty has a private language used only within the group; outsiders, particularly police agents, can then be detected by even a slight linguistic infraction. Appropriate argot denotes a safe person to enter into relations with.[35]

In other words, it is perfectly possible to observe that someone belonging to a different profession is using argot or jargon, but to be unaware that one is doing exactly the same oneself. The fact that 'appropriate argot denotes a safe person to enter into relations with' is as true of sociologists and psychologists as it is of burglars, safe-breakers and racehorse-dopers.

No specialist could fail to recognise a brother and a friend in the masonic clues provided by:

> Just as the articulation of discourse is the revelatory aspect of the document as such, so do we all recognise the need for articulation in the surrogates of documents. It is from this recognition that all the systems of relational factors have arisen; what I hope to present next are some of the surrogational consequences of the foregoing epistemological (or better: alethiological) discussion.[36]

It is probably true to say that the American public is better acquainted than the British with psychological jargon and, on the whole, better disposed towards it. Americans have, for many years accepted psychologists and psychological treatment as a normal feature of their lives, whereas the British still tend to be rather suspicious of them. This means that the average American is more likely to tolerate psychological jargon and even to use it himself, less likely to find it funny or repulsive. Phrases such as 'unrealised potentiality', 'identification with a culture', and 'self-actuating motivation' form part of a way of dealing with human problems which they like and respect. In such matters, expert and layman have, to a considerable extent, come to share the same jargon.

Three Americans and three English people, two men and one women in each case, all belonging to the educated middle class, were asked to read an extract from a popular American book on psychology and to comment on its language and flavour. All the English considered it irritating in different ways, all the Americans found nothing particularly remarkable about it. Three people do not, of course, constitute an adequate statistical sample in either population, but the difference between the two groups is, none the less, interesting.

Here is the passage, which some readers may feel inclined to try out on their friends:

> Consider classical psychoanalysis. The setting is so arranged as to place the analyst out of the visual field of the analysand. This is supposed to allow him to be truly a nonperson. The extent of his presence is supposed to be summed up in the words 'transference' and 'counter-transference'. By remaining a nonperson, the analyst becomes related in the analysand's unconscious to some other person(s) not present in the analytic setting who have been influential in the formation of the analysand's problem. The cure consists of the analysand's working through the transference and accepting, after great resistance, the interpretations which lead to insight. All of this is conceptualized as an intrapsychic process. Add to it the prohibition against social contact with

> the analyst outside the office, the moratorium during which the analysand may make no major life changes, the disinclinations of the analyst to see the analysand's significant others (family, friends, etc.) either with him or without him, and the rather cavalier attitude in psychoanalysis toward what is called 'reality' – and one is left with a therapeutic scheme in which the encapsulated individual struggles with internal conflicting forces in order to achieve mental health.[37]

It is a well-known fact that most people contrive to learn a remarkable number of technical details about the complaints from which they themselves suffer, about the parts of the body which are affected and about the treatment prescribed for them. By listening and repeating, they come to share a little part of the doctor's specialised knowledge. If their illness or indisposition is psychological, and if, as in the United States, they are in the habit of consulting a psychologist or psychiatrist almost as readily as a general practitioner or a specialist in physical ailments, they are very likely to absorb the jargon that belongs to the diagnosis and the treatment. To some extent, the jargon is part of the cure, with a real therapeutic value.

But in order to derive benefit from jargon, which is in this case a form of magic, a degree of fear has to be present and the patient has to long for the magic that will remove the cause of the fear and therefore the fear itself. There is therefore likely to be a fundamental sympathy towards at least some kinds of psychological jargon, those which appear to be linked with mental disturbance. It is quite possible that, for many people, political jargon may have a similar value. If society as one knows it appears unpleasant, uncomfortable or even intolerable, one can very easily find the thought of a political magician attractive. His jargon may not be able to stand up to objective examination, but, if it seems to offer change and the promised land, it will be welcomed.

Economists are not usually considered to be miracle-workers, except possibly by themselves. Years of recession, inflation and unemployment have made most people cynical about economists. The feeling is widespread that, if there is to be a more satisfactory economic future, the key to it is with Fate or the politicians, not with the economists. This means that the jargon used by economists is not felt to possess any magical quality. Like philosophers, economists are increasingly thought of by the general public as irrelevant figures, formulating theories for their own interest and pleasure. Sentences and phrases which contain, one might think, all the qualities required for a successful incantation or charm turn out to have no potency whatever. The priest is left alone to mutter to himself in his temple. An incantation like: 'A single entry in a highly aggregated table may conceal the solid block of a triangular matrix or a narrow strip of finer inter-sectoral relations'[38] arouses no hope in the hearts of the common people, sets no fears at rest. One could put this another way, by saying that during the past quarter of a century economics has ceased to be the humane study which it had once been and has been transformed into a mathematics-based subject. This has inevitably forced economists more and more into a private world from where, like the philosophers, they have very little to say to their fellow citizens. What economists write is read only by other economists. 'Popular' economics is now so difficult a proposition as to be virtually impossible and economists who were trained earlier than 1950 are likely to find incomprehensible what is published nowadays in the name of economics.

How useful economists are to contemporary society is a matter of opinion. The fact that there are a great many of them and that some of the more successful and well-connected occupy well-paid, influential posts in government service proves very little. Their presence, as advisers and senior civil servants, appears to have made remarkably little difference towards solving the two problems which worry people most, inflation and unemployment. It would be difficult for them, under present circumstances, to be greatly loved figures, which is not quite the same as saying that, for most people, economics has fallen into disrepute. A fairer statement would be that economics has retreated into the backroom and that nobody greatly bothers any more.

This is how modern economists talk to one another:

(a) With a great deal of technicality, but no jargon:

> The scheme of ideas comprising a basis-variable, its range of non-revision and the outcome variable whose potential surprise curve is formed by the decision-maker in the light of the recorded values of the basis-variable, provides us with the materials for an insulated dynamic mechanism within the meaning given to this term in chapter IV. A special case of the relationship between basis-variable and outcome variable arises when these two variables are the same in name though differently dated, and when the range of non-revision, say $\vdash\!\dashv x_{1,2}$, formed at date 1 and prescribing the bounds within which x has to fall at date 2 if it is not to engender revision of expectations concerning date 3, is formed in the light of the relation which has emerged at date1 between the value, x_1, then assumed by x and the range of non-revision $\vdash\!\dashv x_{0,1}$ which was entertained up to date 1. Now if x is a market price, we can make assumptions about the particular reaction (to buy or to sell specified quantities, or neither to buy nor sell) of every member of the market, given the relation between the emerging price x_1 and his hitherto entertained range of non-revision $\vdash\!\dashv x_{0,1}$; we can infer the new range of non-revision $\vdash\!\dashv x_{1,2}$, one $\vdash\!\dashv x_{0,1}$ for each member of the market, to which x_1 will give rise; and can also infer the price which will be established at date 2. Then we can suppose the viewpoint to be at date 2 and can

observe the new, date 2, relation between price and previous range of non-revision for each member of the market; we can again infer his selling or buying reaction and his new range of non-revision $\vdash\!\dashv x_{2,3}$; and so on.[39]

(b) With a small amount of technicality and a great deal of jargon:

For example, suppose each male regarded the affection of the one female as yielding equal incremental utility relative to incremental utility yielded by affection of the other male. Optimality would result from pairwise optimality only if the female regarded affection from either of the two males as equally good at the margin! This could happen if goods can substitute for affection as shown in Theorem 3. Otherwise further rules of exchange would have to supplement pairwise optimality in order to ensure Pareto optimality. It therefore appears that the equivalence of pairwise optimality and efficiency is restricted to more or less the cases that include classical economic exchange in private commodities.

The above example should not be confused with the marriage game (Gale and Shapley (5)) which is a game with indivisibilities. It happens that the equivalence of pairwise optimality and efficiency holds in the marriage game, and thus there is still some small hope for extending the equivalence theorem vis-à-vis general social systems.[40]

(c) With an equal amount of technicality and jargon:

We shall hypothesize that encounters on the trail and in camp affect an individual's willingness to pay for a given wilderness experience. This hypothesis follows from the Lancaster model previously developed. Consider a change in the amount of solitude provided to a recreationist in a given trip to a wilderness area. Such a change will be measured in terms of the number of encounters experienced during the trip. If A_1 represents solitude, then increased use of any wilderness area in a given time interval will increase the likelihood of encounters experienced by a particular party (Stankey (18), pp 106–108) and thereby reduce the perceived solitude. In terms of Figure 1, if x_3 measures the amount of wilderness recreation effects on solitude can be represented by a clockwise pivoting of OX_3. In terms of Equation (7) the quantity of A_1 provided by a unit of x_3 (i.e. b_{13}) is reduced. Hence the demand price or willingness to pay (P_3) for wilderness recreation will also be less than before the change in the attribute (solitude) provided.[41]

It is difficult to think of any piece of jargon more dreadful than 'the amount of wilderness recreation consumed', although the notion that affection can yield incremental utility runs it very close. Such writing is both corrupt and corrupting, and it is small consolation to know that it is, as yet, rarely produced by British economists, however eager they may be to be well regarded by their American colleagues.

One point must be made in defence of today's economists. It is not their fault that most people who call themselves educated are so grossly and shamefully ignorant of mathematics and statistics. They are under no obligation to make their work intelligible to a public which is not numerate. But they certainly have a duty, both to civilisation and to themselves, to stop talking about 'the amount of wilderness recreation consumed' and 'the equivalence of pairwise optimality and efficiency in the marriage game'.

Much less harmful and, in its way, even charming is the remark made to the present author by a professor of economics a few years ago in a public house. He would, he said, be grateful for a short-term loan of a pound, since he was 'temporarily short of liquidity'.

5 The Would-be Professions

'The insurance profession'; 'the profession of banking'; 'the advertising profession'; 'the profession of journalism'; 'the accountancy profession'; 'the profession of management' – the list of occupations claiming to be professions is a lengthening one and the rights and wrongs of the matter have been argued in the introductory chapter to this book. We shall concentrate here on two groups of people, the advertisers and those concerned with business management, who are each responsible for a formidable amount of jargon each year.

In 1875, when Henry Sampson published his pioneering *History of Advertising*, American businessmen were beginning to sell their goods by methods which seemed crude and repulsive to many of those who had been reared in the more solid and respectable traditions of British commerce. 'With very few exceptions,' wrote Sampson, 'the papers which come from the United States – we refer not to the hole and corner, but to the high class, which are widely read and disseminated among family circles – contain advertisements which would be rejected by the gutter journals of this country.'[1]

It appears that Sampson's particular dislikes were American 'suggestiveness' and the slang words and phrases that occurred so frequently in the advertisements. It is clear, too, that the American copy-writers favoured a more vigorous and dramatic technique than was normal in Britain. They saw no reason why they should not be sensational on occasion – after all, they were trying to sell goods to pioneers, immigrants and self-made men, not to the English middle and upper classes. America was not England, much as the offended British might pretend otherwise.

Sampson was reacting in a normal Victorian manner, but it is rather odd that, with such a wealth of carefully collected evidence in his files, he should have failed to notice that, even in the eighteenth century, there had been more than one tradition of advertising in Britain and that, at any period, people with goods and services to sell will use the kind of language which seems appropriate to their potential customers.

Salesmen and advertisers must, of necessity, be exceptionally interested in the possibilities of words. Their sole task is to extol the merits and conceal the weaknesses of whatever it is that they are trying to sell. This means, and always has, that they must be prepared to exaggerate, and therefore, to deceive. There is nothing particularly startling or immoral in this. The public has always expected sales-talk to be biased. A purely objective commercial advertisement, whether in print, on the screen or by word of mouth, is a contradiction in terms. The advertiser, like the politician, cannot be expected to give disinterested advice, and the sensible citizen will accordingly remember the Latin tag, *caveat emptor*, and keep his wits about him. The more continuous and determined the sales-talk becomes, the more he is obliged either to ignore it or to build up his defences against it. He cannot buy everything, he cannot vote for all the candidates, he cannot sympathise with all causes, however assiduously he is wooed. To protect himself against the never-ending assault on his needs, his loyalties and his pocket, he has to develop a way of automatically rejecting most of the appeals which are made to him. In the process of learning this survival technique, he is likely to become more cynical, more suspicious, less capable of enthusiasm. Twentieth-century man spends a good deal of his life within his shell, because so many people with a living to earn are trying to get at him and eat him.

There are, of course, self-righteous denials of this by firms who advertise a great deal. Some of them make interesting reading, for instance: 'The suggestion by some publicists that the shopper is engaged in a constant battle of wits with the manufacturer, and thus needs protection against his or her inability to make a wise purchase, is certainly not true of the product sold under advertised brands.'[2] The success of consumer organisations and of magazines such as *Which*? is strong evidence that the battle of wits is felt by the public at large to be a very real thing.

Despite changes in the economic and social pattern of English life, more particularly the gradual increase in the purchasing power of the artisan and lower middle classes, the general tone of advertising remained quiet and conservative during the whole of the nineteenth century. The more popular, aggressive, dramatic advertisements, when they eventually came, were the product of a new, mass-readership type of journalism, improved and cheaper methods of printing illustrations, and a steady rise in the number of people with a little money left in their pockets each week after the bare necessities of life had been paid for.

Some commodities have never really left the old advertising style behind. Houses are a good example. A house advertisement of a hundred years ago was a sober and dignified piece of prose, offering such attractions as 'a large and well-stocked wall-garden and a lawn of about two acres, belted by a three foot wide and mostly gravelled walk, and bounded by a clear stream of running water about ten feet wide and two feet deep, with a beautiful and romantic view of the opposite hills and woods'. A century later the hook is still being baited with the same kind of phrase; 'a supremely quiet and exclusive private drive with fine all-round views.; 'standing in a fine position amidst a wealth of magnificent trees, overlooking undulating meadows and the River Trent'; 'a secluded haven of real beauty'.

But the social context of such language has changed. The house-agent, the wine-merchant and the furniture-maker of 1850 were selling to people who really did possess considerable means and leisure; their successors nowadays are fully aware of the commercial importance of flattering a client to believe that he has the money, taste and position of a past age. The 'gracious-living' of the English upper-classes of the eighteenth and nineteenth centuries is brought from its grave in order to provide the late twentieth century with something with which to build its dreams and myths. The modern estate agent often uses this technique in a completely shameless manner. His snob-appeal sometimes has a ludicrous aspect to it. He is so anxious to project house-hunters back into the past that he is liable, deliberately or accidentally, to forget his history and to offer an 'Elizabethan cottage (1644), oak beamed', or to blend several fashionable and desirable architectural styles together in his advertised description of the property.

A few years ago the present author noticed an advertisement which announced that the agent had 'an applicant wanting a house with a nice type of architecture'. Nice people obviously deserve a nice type of architecture. Other much-used phrases with the same overtones are 'this favoured neighbourhood' and 'the properties are admired by all who know them'.

It is easy to tilt at the estate agents and it has been done often enough. Their odd jargon has become part of the English way of life. It is supposed to be effective. Houses, we are told, would not sell so well without its aid.[3] Yet during the 1950s and 1960s one pioneering firm[4] in London, whose enterprising proprietor is now unfortunately dead, achieved great success by adopting scandalously original tactics. Instead of speaking about clients and houses in the respectful manner which had become traditional, it poked fun at them. Readers of the Sunday newspapers with no intention of buying a house found a great deal of pleasure in these delicious advertisements, which were enlivened by such remarks as 'Underpaid English Diplomat and his Lady ask us . . .'; 'Décor jolly good and, of course, Regency'; 'Schoolmaster and Actress emigrating to Canada'; 'Extremely respectable 1905 villa residence in Chiswick, which is coming up in the world'.

Estate agents of the old school put pressure on the newspapers to prevent these advertisements from appearing. The threat to their own established style and approach was too obvious. Anyone who prospered by satirising his fellows was a menace to good order and had to be suppressed. The dignity of the profession – if the public was to be persuaded to think of it as a profession – was imperilled by such advertisements as: 'Cheap big flat. High and sunny. Gorgeous view over River and Boat Race. Ammonia liqueur Magnate (The new aperitif?) and girl scion of the Sinn Fein suddenly going North. Already spent £300 on rewiring, but some decor still has air of Dickensian squalor.'[5] and 'Flat for sale. Bolton Gardens, S. Ken., S.W.5., 1st Flr. Use, I think, of the gdn. sq. Large Drawing rm. 2 decent enough bedrooms, b. and k. pretty grim at the moment, but what on earth do you expect in an area where postwar Rolls are parked by the kerb, for £1,500.'[6]

The rebel had no successors. Other house-agents on both sides of the Atlantic regard houses as too sacred for laughter and persevere with the traditional 'town house of character', 'one of Esher's loveliest Small Houses', 'Only wants seeing', and the rest of the dreary collection of platitudes. Yet this jargon is something more than absurd. It prevents thought and discrimination and it keeps the public mind looking perpetually backwards. When a Victorian advertised a house as 'fit for the residence of a respectable family', or said it was 'genteelly furnished', he was using a fairly exact terminology, which reflected the tastes and social structure of Victorian England. He was not merely stringing words together in the interests of a good sale. Nowadays, so many of the once-meaningful words, like 'reception room', 'breakfast room', 'hall with cloaks', and 'weekend residence' have withered away into nonsense, because nobody, apart from royalty and millionaires, still lives in such a fashion. Yet the weaker the old status symbols become in reality, the more easily people can be conditioned to want them as part of their day-dreaming kit. By a skilful blending of words and pictures the most unlikely persons can be persuaded to identify themselves with the best people. They are hypnotised.

The cruise-advertisers are masters at the art of hypnosis. They can promote 'the most sought-after quality cruises from New York'[7] by skilfully suggesting, without needing to say so explicitly, that the cruises are sought after by the richest and most socially desirable people. They promise 'high cruise standards, enhanced by a dedicated Italian crew',[8] without indicating whether the crew are dedicated to their work, the captain, the shipping line, the passengers, or to the extraction of large tips. In pre-1914 days, the wealthy and the aristocratic had dedicated servants; the tradition is continued, for those able to find the money, by a dedicated Italian crew on a cruising liner.

One is asked to identify oneself with many different kinds of people from the past, all distinguished. The following cruise advertisement is worth studying carefully, both for its total effect and its details.

> FEEL THE EXHILARATION OF THE GREAT EXPLORERS –
>
> Reach out and touch the monuments of ancient Egypt. Join a safari through the finest game preserves of Africa. Gaze on Kilimanjaro and the incredible carved churches of Ethopia. Visit remote towns on the Arabian Peninsula which will soon end their centuries of isolation.
>
> See the jewel-like cities of the Persian Empire, the tiled domes of

Isfahan, the painted caves and sculptures of India and Ceylon. Behold the Taj Mahal and sail into the amazing harbours of Rangoon, Singapore, Bangkok and Hong Kong. Explore the temples of Java and sway with the exotic dancers of Bali.

These are some of the possibilities for those able to join us this winter aboard thc perfect space and comfort of the MTS Daphne.[9]

The cruises in question last for either 45 or 89 days, and they are extremely expensive. 'Those able to join us' is a clever phrase, containing two flattering concepts – 'those who can afford to come' and 'those who are able to snatch the time from a very busy life'. 'Join us' gives the right impression of a house party or a cruise on a private yacht. The travel-agent's jargon is well represented here – 'the monuments of ancient Egypt', 'the finest game preserves of Africa', 'the incredible carved churches of Ethopia', 'centuries of isolation', 'jewel-like cities', 'tiled domes', 'exotic dancers of Bali'. The tourist is being given a series of orders, which he is conditioned to carry out not merely willingly, but eagerly. He is told – the imperative mood of the verb is used throughout – to 'reach out', 'touch', 'join', 'gaze', 'visit', 'see', 'behold' and 'explore', and precisely what he is to visit is laid down in advance. Nothing is left to his own initiative. He pays for clichés and he gets them. The colour slides he brings home are almost certain to reflect this. Everybody is in the conspiracy together, a band of brothers who have sworn a jargon-oath.

'To inoculate the few who influence the many is the *Atlantic's* perpetual formula', said one of the *Atlantic Monthly's* great editors, Ellery Sedgewick, and the same might well be said of the other 'quality' magazines, notably *Harper's*, *Vogue* and the *New Yorker*. The process by which ideas and opinions filter downwards through the social classes is of great importance to advertisers and every opportunity is taken to encourage it. But it is too slow and too unpredictable to be allowed to act on its own. The market has to be hit directly and further down at the same time. In his book, *Social Class in America*, published in 1948, Lloyd Warner divided the Americans into six social classes. Of these, the top three were reckoned to contain 15 per cent of the population and to make up the 'quality market'. It is, however, as Vance Packard pointed out, 'the fourth and fifth classes that fascinate merchandisers, because they constitute, together, about sixty-five per cent of the population in a typical community and make up a great concentration of the nation's purchasing power. Merchandisers have been particularly interested in the female of the species in the sixty-five per cent of the population. They call her Mrs Middle Majority'.[10]

One can therefore say, assuming that something like a figure of 65 per cent applies to other parts of the English-speaking world as well, that advertising language can be divided socially in approximately the following way:

> *Category A* Aimed at the top 15 per cent and characterised by sophistication, understatement, suggestion and allusion.
> *Category B* Aimed at the middle 65 per cent, who tend to be less confident than Category A, more frightened of doing the wrong thing. On the other hand, they are quite likely to admire the money and the lifestyle of those in Category A and to buy such versions of Category A goods and services as they can afford.

One can try to appeal to each category of people separately and specially, but it is impossible to guarantee that what is written for one group will not be read by members of the other. People in doctors' and dentists' waiting-rooms, for example, are likely to leaf through magazines which are both above and below their usual level, and they may pick up a good deal of new and perhaps surprising information as a result. Television commercials, on the other hand, can be reckoned to be aimed almost entirely at the 65 per cent.

The jargon in the following passage is quite clearly for Category A, the 15 per cent.

> Parure. It is a word which is difficult to translate. One could say 'ornament' or 'adornment', but one would be missing the point. It is 'ornament' only in the sense of a jeweled ornament from Tiffany's. It is 'adornment', but in the sense of an aura, creating presence which is *felt* more than seen. Parure is a fragrance of exquisite femininity. A fragrance evoking a season of lilacs and plums, the vigor of cypress, the charm of amber. It is lingering, opulent. And stunning. It is a perfume that says exactly what you want it to say.[11]

This is an interesting example of what Geoffrey N. Leech calls 'strategic semantics'.[12] He defines 'strategic semantics' as 'the art of conveying meanings which contribute to the selling effectiveness of an advertisement, and avoiding those which detract from it.'[13] There are a number of ways in which this can be achieved. One is to be deliberately vague. The passage about Parure, quoted above, is very skilfully vague from beginning to end. It shifts the burden of definition from the seller to the purchaser. 'Parure,' it says, 'says exactly what you want it to say', whatever that might be, and no perfume could be more obliging than that.

Another way of making the public do all the work is what Mr Leech has named 'disjunctive copy', that is, not writing in complete sentences, in order to encourage the reader's imagination to work hard at the full stops. Supposing, he says, we take as our example:

> Kellogg's Frosties. So crisp and refreshing. Sparkling with a snowy

sugar frosting. Toasted to a golden crispness. Kellogg's Frosties. The crisp breakfast.

The effect, he notes, is quite different if we decide to fill in the missing verbs and pronouns, and to reword the advertisement like this:

Kellogg's Frosties are so crisp and refreshing. They sparkle with a snowy sugar frosting and they are toasted to a golden crispness. Kellogg's Frosties are the crisp breakfast.

The second version sounds even more banal than the first, but that, from the point of view of the expert, is not the main or the most important difference. The power to stimulate associations has been removed by telling the reader too much. In the original version, he is compelled to pause five times between 'Kellogg's' and 'breakfast' and at each point he should, at least in theory, be having thoughts which are good for the advertiser's business. Or, as Geoffrey Leech puts it: 'Disjunctive copy communicates at a sub-logical level and helps in the reinforcement of the associative as opposed to the cognitive side of the message.'[14]

This is a comparatively modern technique, so far as advertising is concerned, although poets have used it for centuries. That it works there can be no doubt, but whether it sells any more goods is open to question. The advertiser has to believe it does, however; what he believes he is doing is to feed his customers with sufficient clichés about his product to make reasonably sure that what one might call their free thoughts take off in the right direction. This produces an interesting situation, in which the public is personally involved in writing the advertisement by filling in the blanks from a carefully induced dreamworld. An important aspect of advertising jargon consists of its power to make reasonably sure that the dreamworld is controlled in a way which is like to benefit sales. Hostile, critical dreams are certainly not to be encouraged.

The kind of day-dreaming which builds mental bridges between oneself and the great and well-born – Lord Lichfield and the Burberry raincoat – has had a long run for its money in Britain and indeed in most countries of the Capitalist West, although the possession of a royal family and an abundance of hereditary titles gives Britain a great advantage over its rivals. The style of this kind of advertising has changed considerably, however. Before about 1920 it was common enough to find goods advertised as having been supplied at some time or other to members of the Royal Family, the Duke of X or the Earl of Y. This was quite openly done and served merely as a guarantee of the standing of the firm and the quality of the goods, although some of these early associations with Royalty read a little oddly nowadays. In 1790, for instance, we find a certain Dr Harvey advertising his 'Anti venereal Pills' as being 'By his Majesty's Royal Authority', and sold 'on the principle of no cure, no Pay'.[15] The distinguished patrons were kept firmly in the background, however. There were no pictures of King Edward VII wearing Smith's boots, and certainly none of the Countess of M. having her hair done at Jones's.

During the 1920s and 1930s a rather lighter and more subtle touch began to be noticeable. 'The discerning few' were both the target and the means of attack. One had the Royal Arms at the top of the advertisement and underneath merely 'wherever fine cigarettes are appreciated, smokers choose . . .' Or, Prince Charles Edward looking on approvingly at a fireside gathering of elegantly dressed people, while the text announces that 'Drambuie brings the richness of the past to the appreciative palate. Since the days of Prince Charles Edward Stuart, when the secret of this exquisite liqueur was first brought to Scotland, it has become a favourite throughout the world with persons of discrimination', with whom the reader was expected to immediately identify himself.

The English tradition, exploited by the advertisers, is that English gentlemen and gentlewomen leave extravagant language, like extravagant habits in general, to Americans, foreigners and vulgar people wherever they may be found. The high social prestige of a product can therefore be identified merely by using words which are exceptionally simple and modest. A car is described as good, a shoe as fine, and an apéritif as the best. So one has become accustomed to the kind of advertisement which shows a Georgian – genuine Georgian – doorway, and underneath, 'Behind this door . . . in an elegant setting, refreshment is being taken and pleasure given. Here, the best of all orange drinks – Jaffajuice – is naturally at home in a world where good taste and good things abound.[16]

The language melts into the picture. Jargon words are supported by cliché pictures, to create a wonderful, never-never world in which there is no ugliness, no misery and no brutality, and, most important of all, where everyone has enough money for all their needs and all their luxuries. But what are consumers in fact buying when they respond to an advertisement? Not merely commodities with physical properties, but subjective satisfactions as well. It is this which makes the efforts of consumer advisory services to some degree irrelevant. Nobody thinks well of a motor car which breaks down or of curtain material which fades rapidly, but people will not necessarily buy what objective tests prove to offer the best value for money. For certain kinds of goods and services, satisfaction is a complicated matter. It can be achieved by having something that large numbers of people have got and also by having something which is in the possession of only a very few. The value can be intrinsic, as with a diamond, or almost wholly as a result of pleasant associations, as with a bottle of perfume or a restaurant meal. The advertisers know perfectly well that, for a large part of their time, they are appealing to the irrational and they depend very largely on this for their success.

> Spring. It does a lot for your skin, but it can't do everything.
>
> It's not just the trees that blossom in Springtime.
>
> Everything seems to look better, including your complexion. But the real secret is to catch that improvement and help it just a little bit more by using Oil of Ulay Beauty Fluid. Oil of Ulay is a very special blend of tropical-moist oils, that replaces vital oils and moisture in a unique and natural way. Keeping your skin looking as youthful and smooth as it should.[17]

Slightly exaggerated, maybe, and with one or two phrases which it is better not to examine too closely, if one wishes to retain one's faith in the miracle-working qualities of Oil of Ulay. Who or what is Ulay? What does 'tropical-moist' mean? How can something that comes out of a bottle and has to be rubbed into the skin be described as natural? But the notion of perpetual youth is a pleasant fiction that does nobody any harm.

Consider the language and form of a selection of recent advertisements from this point of view.

There is in the Haymarket, London, a double-fronted tobacconists's shop, belonging to Fribourg and Treyer, which has preserved its eighteenth century bow-windows. Above the windows is a notice which tells the passer-by that Fribourg and Treyer were 'Purveyors to their Majesties the Kings of Hanover and Belgium and his Royal Highness the Duke of Cambridge'. On the door is painted 'Founded in 1720.'

An advertisement published in 1976[18] has a pleasant little drawing of the shop at the top of the page and underneath a heading, 'We are not yet ready to join the Machine Age', and then a few lines of text, which read:

> As a service to clients we are seeking to make our No. 1 Filter de Luxe obtainable in places other than the Haymarket shop. To this end, an American visitor suggested we might use a cigarette machine.
>
> On investigation we found the machine unable to change a tenner, accept a cheque, give street directions or make sanguine guesses at the Ascot weather and provide the other services our clients have come to expect.
>
> We have, instead, appointed additional select outlets to serve your cigarettes personally.

A photograph of a discreetly half-opened box of cigarettes and the job was done, the obligatory 'Every packet carries a Government health warning' making a rather ludicrous postscript.

This advertisement is very obviously not aimed at a mass market. The *Illustrated London News*, in which the advertisement appeared, is not that kind of periodical. Fribourg and Treyer sell their cigarettes, cigars and tobacco by emphasising that they do everything in the old way. They have clients, not customers, they deal with people who make their purchases in a leisurely fashion, pay for them with ten-pound notes and cheques, and go to Ascot each year as a matter of course. People with a strong democratic urge who dislike this sort of thing are free to say that the advertisement, like the firm, is élitist and written in upper-class jargon. If conservative English, containing no colloquial contractions and no slang, is now jargon, the criticism must be accepted. But – and the point is an important one – everything in the advertisement is fully intelligible. No word or phrase in it could baffle even the most ferociously hostile critic. The writer may, it is true, be telling his intended audience what it wants to hear in a manner which is acceptable to them, but this is evidence of skill and sensitivity. He is communicating and that, as yet, is not a criminal offence, however much one may dislike what is being communicated and the people at whom it is directed.

A little further down the social ladder is a double-page colour supplement[19] spread produced for the United States Travel Service, to draw attention to the attractions of New Orleans. It says all the usual things, but it says them enthusiastically, and with plenty of semantic disjunction.

> For a start, New Orleans is the city of joie de vivre. With its carnivals, processions and famous Fat Tuesday, the Mardi Gras.
>
> Then there are the surrounding sights.
>
> The old Mississippi rolling along. Steamboats. Listen! There's the sound of the 'Delta Queen'. Honking. Churning water. Heading down the river.
>
> Antebellum mansions. The Cottage Plantation. Where you can sleep in a four-poster bed. And have hominy grits for breakfast.
>
> In the lush heart of Louisiana.
>
> Quaint villages. Country dances on a Saturday night. The French two-step. To the rhythm of accordions, fiddles and a Cajun song.
>
> The bayous and the rivers. Flowing down to the Gulf of Mexico. Soak in the semi-tropical sea, with the dolphins and flying fish. And bikini-clad mermaids. Smile for your snapshot.

What is one reading here? Do 'city of joie de vivre', 'the lush heart of Louisiana', 'quaint villages' and the rest belong to the jargon of the advertising industry or the jargon of the tourist industry? Is advertising like an actor, with no face of its own, but only that of the part it happens to be playing at the moment? The second possibility seems the more likely. An advertising specialist asks his client, in effect, three questions:

1. What exactly is it that we are trying to sell together?
2. What are its original, different, outstanding, saleable characteristics?
3. What ideas and phrases does the public commonly associate with this particular commodity?

Without needing himself to be particularly astute or inventive, he may discover that the subject of the advertisement has a jargon firmly attached to it in the public mind. He then has to decide whether to follow this jargon, modify it, give it a slightly different flavour, or abandon it and try something completely different. He must, so to speak, feel his way into the part that has been given to him. He can certainly advise and guide his client as to the current state of the public's prejudice, needs, fear and snobbery. He has, or should have, access to the latest psychological knowledge concerning such matters as motivation, suggestibility and resistance to pressure, and he will use this experience to his client's advantage. But what he cannot do is to arrive on the job with a ready-made repertoire of style and jargon and proceed to enrich the task of the moment with it, like currants in a cake. In this sense, there is no such thing as a single advertising jargon; there are hundreds.

One job will produce this jargon:

> Put your decorating thumb to work in your big high-ceilinged bedroom and see it burst into bloom with all the exuberance of your showplace garden. Grow larger-than-life dogwood (daisies, anemones or geraniums if you'd rather) everywhere . . . after all, the ceiling's the limit. And bring it all into beautiful balance with the fine-woods complement of furniture scales for your room.[20]

and another this:

> A fantastic offer of seeds and bulbs of gorgeous exciting plants from around the world. Novelties, rarities, re-discovered treasures. The wonders of nature you read about but never know where to find. From lovely border, bedding and rockery plants, beautiful trees and shrubs, to the rarest and most exotic greenhouse and pot plants. Ferns, Bonsai, Fly-eaters, Cacti, Orchids, and novelties for flower arrangers, and mouth-watering fruit and vegetable specialities. Something new, something exciting for every gardener anywhere in the world.[21]

No kind of advertising anywhere in the English-speaking world contains as much jargon – often incomprehensible jargon – at the present time as that produced to recruit management staff. Here, to begin with, are three better-than-average examples.

> Our client is a member of one of the country's most successful international organisations operating within the ethos of decentralisation and profit responsibility. The company manufactures and sells a range of high-quality durables.
> Due to retirement, a vacancy exists in the top management team for a Sales Director whose main task will be the continuation of profitable market expansion that has emanated from aggressive marketing and development policies . . . . A comprehensive remuneration package will be offered and relocation assistance will be given should this be necessary.[22]

> After a period of induction training concentrated on user and large account selling, you will assume complete responsibility for the export sales management control function which you will set up against marketing guidelines and report directly to the managing director. You will recognise the company commitment to a philosophy of profitable sales attainment consistent with company marketing policy and production capacity.[23]

> Our client is an international leader in the consumer goods industry and manufactures a wide range of quality products. They [sic] are seeking to appoint an ambitious person to augment a compact and dynamic corps of Sales Team Leaders currently being developed to fill key positions in Field Sales Management before the middle of 1976. Applicants should possess a sound background in planned selling techniques and a proven success record within a national consumer goods environment. Inherent commercial acumen and natural leadership qualities are important and candidates will probably already have been identified as management development material or have achieved sales supervisory level in their present companies.[24]

The recruitment agencies, in fairness to them, are not the original source of this jargon. It has become part of the atmosphere of the international business world and the management schools. The agencies simply pick it up and string it together. By being in constant touch with business the agency people find it no problem to produce dreadful sentences like 'You will recognise the company commitment with company marketing policy and production capacity'. It is important to notice that not only do businessmen write pompous rubbish like this, they speak it as well. During 1974 the chairman of a large British engineering concern was asked, in the course of a television interview, what he felt the main problem of his company to be at that time. He replied that it was 'to generate the availability of exposure of our management'. The interviewer did not enquire what this remarkable sentence might mean and one can only guess. Somewhere in the background there was probably a quite simple thought, such as 'We're trying to persuade our managers to make themselves more accessible and better-known to the people they control', but the pressure to sound dignified and impressive, professional and important, prevented it from coming to the surface in this form. There appears to be a deeply-felt inner need to grade up business, so that the everyday activities of making and selling things shall seem not only respectable but noble and God-given. Simple, concrete, colloquial language is felt to be inferior and even low.

There is clearly a circular process at work. Businessmen talk like the advertisements and the advertisements talk like businessmen. Each has a corrupting effect on the other. The annual crop of company reports is worth studying in this connection.

> Tiptoe on the misty mountain top [announced the Morgan Crucible Company in its 1974 report]. We would never have scaled the profit peak of 1974 without the whole-hearted co-operation of all our people throughout the world. There are further peaks in the mountain range to be scaled but, given the present state of world trade, we will certainly pause for breath in 1975. Even the chamois must on occasion stop before again leaping forward. Although it is hard to see through the swirling mists of the immediate future, it remains as true as ever that Morgan is uniquely placed to take advantage of any general economic revival, and more particularly the accelerating demand for energy conservation in the developed world and for basic industrialisation in the developing world; poised, like the chamois, for the next sure-footed leap upwards.

The language of this prose-poem has an hypnotic effect. Well-hidden in in the middle of all this mountain and chamois talk is the basic, but hardly encouraging message, '1975 is going to be a stagnant year, with no growth at all'. The whole passage is either a clever confidence-trick or a splendid piece of morale-building, according to one's point of view.

The soil in which business jargon grows is formed by the inability or refusal to use simple language.[25] Close contact with the business world for many years has given the present author a much-valued opportunity to observe this inhibition in action. One develops the habit of first noting what is actually said and then thinking of the translation. The double-entry system produces this kind of result:

Words actually used	*Suggested translation*
We aim at buyer-satisfaction	We want the people who buy our goods to be satisfied
The conversion operation is of limited duration	It doesn't take long to convert our equipment
We shall review the validity of the maps	We'll check to make sure the maps are up-to-date
There is a shortage of bedspace in the Metropolis	It's difficult to find a hotel room in London
On initial arrival at the hotel	When we got to the hotel
Basically, we are endeavouring to	We're trying to

What is nowadays euphemistically called 'industry' and used to be known without shame or embarrassment by the blunt old-fashioned name of 'manufacturing' goes to a great deal of trouble to avoid using crude words like 'factory', 'site', or 'working conditions'. 'Environment' is a popular alternative, as the following examples show:

> . . . a Senior Planning Engineer who has a background in a light or heavy engineering environment[26]
>
> The environment is fast-moving and structured[27]
>
> Ideally you should have worked in an overseas environment[28]

Another much-favoured word for 'factory' is 'facility', as in 'Ardbrook, which has recently relocated to a new facility at Livingston, Scotland . . .'[29] Goods are no better for being made in a facility, but the change is apparently beneficial to the morale of the people employed there.

In the old days, a company's products were distributed and there was a Distribution Manager or a Transport Manager to make sure that the task was properly carried out. This is so no longer. The person responsible for this aspect of the firm's activities is known as Manager, Physical Distribution, although the small print in the advertisements makes clear that he has precisely the same duties as ever – 'Applicants must have a wide range of experience, covering importing, freight, warehousing, transport and distribution throughout U.K.'[30] What the company's non-physical distribution may consist of we are left to guess.

'Function' is another word which is felt to add dignity to the duties carried on by the various branches of industrial management. Usually, it can be struck out of the sentence with no loss of meaning whatever. In one case, 'the successful applicant should have had experience in the accounting function'.[31] In another, the person appointed 'will be responsible for developing an effective training function'[32], and in a third the post is 'due to reorganisation of the engineering function'.[33]

In the first instance, 'experience in the accounting function' means 'experience in accounting'; in the second, 'an effective training function' is 'an effective training department'; and in the third, 'the engineering function' is 'the engineering department'. Exactly why the first expression should be preferred to the second in these instances is not clear, since there is nothing particularly disreputable or sordid about accounting, training or engineering. Modern business likes to give the impression, however, that it is a carefully structured affair, with everybody's 'function' clearly defined and organised. It is just possible that people throw out their chests and work harder and more loyally if they are told that they have a function, rather than just a job, but if this is indeed the case industrial management must contain some pretty naive people.

Another grossly over-worked industrial[34] word is 'self-starter'. Broadly speaking, there are two types of employee nowadays. The first has to be pushed, kicked and continuously supervised if any work is to be got out of him at all, and the second, every employer's dream, is the person who does things on his own initiative, without needing to receive a string of orders. This is the self-starter. So, one company will lay down, without realising the implications of the second part of the sentence, 'You must be an enthusiastic self-starter, preferably with a motor manufacturer'[35] A second, perhaps optimistically, suggests that 'the ideal applicant must be a self-starter'[36]; and the third evidently feels that someone even more anxious to work 'must be a strongly motivated self-starter'.[37]

'Motivated', 'self-motivated' and 'self-motivating' have become key words in today's industrial world. Managers are supposed to be able to 'motivate' their staff, which means, roughly speaking, to persuade them to do a reasonable day's work, but the élite of the labour market are supposed to possess inner drives which render outside assistance and encouragement unnecessary. A salesman must therefore be 'totally self-motivating and able to operate from a home base'[38] and a research engineer, less grammatically, has to possess 'the ability to self-motivate'.[39]

One cannot, unfortunately, assume that any great amount of thought goes into the preparation of this kind of advertisement. Many of them, indeed, suggest that someone has put his hand into a bag full of possible phrases, pulled out what seems to be about the right number and assembled them to form a piece of continuous, winning prose. What is much worse is that managerial people do actually use such words in what passes among them for conversation. They really do say that X is a self-starter and that Y is self-motivated, although most of them would probably stop short of asking a prospective colleague, 'Do you have the ability to self-motivate?', which is still reserved for the written language.

Industry sets great store on the members of its managerial staff being dynamic – 'our dynamic Chairman' – and 'involved'. The latter is today's word for the company man, the person who thinks about his job 24 hours a day. So the new man 'must have personality for executive involvement in publicly quoted company'[40] and two high-ranking pieces of jargon come together when 'complete job involvement is required from a self-starter who . . .'[41]

'Interface' originally and properly was a technical term, meaning the connection of one piece of apparatus with another. It is now enormously and infuriatingly used to mean 'liaison' or 'co-operation', which can be substituted for 'interface' in the following and most other examples.

> There is a strong M.O.D.[42] interface[43]

> Our understanding of the interface between schools and higher education[44]

> A direct interface with design engineering will be required to aid in resolving assembly and design related problems.[45]

It is difficult to imagine how the world managed before the word 'executive' came into common use. A foolproof definition is not easy. To say that an executive is a person who earns a living from administration of some kind is tempting but inadequate. The closest one can get to it, perhaps, is to suggest that the label can be attached to anyone in a white-collar job who is in a position to give orders to other people. The number of such subordinates is immaterial. It can be two, it can be two thousand.

The word is used in its most reasonable and understandable sense in the description of a town as 'a busy commercial centre, with many business executives, from home and abroad, passing through regularly'.[46] But, used as an adjective, 'executive' poses problems. We have, for example, 'this truly unique executive resort';[47] '2 pairs of executive slacks for only 19.55';[48] and, to crown everything, 'Executive fix-it. A 5" high hammer for making small on-the-spot repairs, plus a knife, screw-driver, ruler and pick. All to make you the hero of the office.'[49]

An 'executive resort' is presumably a holiday centre patronised by members of the executive class, that is, by people with a certain predictable level of income, but what 'executive slacks' can be is far from clear. What is it that makes a pair of trousers specially and peculiarly suitable for an executive? Is it their price, cut, material, or what? And an 'executive fix-it' defies the best efforts of the imagination. Anybody is entitled to be 'the hero of the office', but why should the man in charge be expected to be the odd-job man as well? Why should he want to be? The explanation in this case is that probably the executive is the person most likely to be reading the in-flight magazine in which this particular gadget is advertised, so that some reason, however far-fetched and whimsical, has to be devised to explain why he should spend his money in this curious way.

'Generous' is now an obligatory word in business where holidays and removal expenses are concerned. One word is practically never used without the other. Examples, chosen at random, are: 'generous holiday entitlement'[50] and 'generous relocation expenses'.[51]

At one time it was a recommendation, when applying for a new post, to have had experience of this or that branch of the work. This is so no longer. One is now exposed to something, one does not have experience of it. So we learn that 'the position . . . will appeal to a person who preferably but not necessarily has been exposed to the Ford range of parts and accessories'.[52]

One can, of course, be exposed to a particular kind of work without learning anything as a result or without showing the slightest aptitude for it. The most stupid and unteachable person in the world can be exposed to the Ford range of parts for months and years without being any the wiser.

Both jobs and companies have 'high visibility', although the precise meaning of the term is sometimes open to doubt. 'Rising well above the rank-and-file' is perhaps the nearest one can get to a general interpretation. Here are two typical examples: 'High visibility corporate';[53] 'This high-visibility position with advancement potential'.[54]

Business finds it difficult to the use the words 'big' and 'small'. The reason for this inhibition seems to be that few firms can be sure that they are the biggest – how big is big? – and nobody wishes to be considered small. To overcome any possible embarrassment, a number of alternatives are in common use. 'Major' is the favourite substitute for 'big'. 'This French subsidiary of a major international company';[55] 'A major hospital products subsidiary'.[56] 'Major' has two advantages over 'big'. It does not cause one to ask 'how big?' and it conveys the notion of importance as well as size.

'Limited' has been found to be a very acceptable replacement for 'small', not only because it avoids the crude word, but because it also suggests 'deliberately restricted in number', 'select'. The Bicentennial carpet is now being shown at a limited number of fine stores;[57] and a retailing group 'has a limited number of vacancies in its buying team.'[58]

'Substantial' is another handy jargon word, keeping the size of something conveniently vague and adding a sense of solidity to the total concept. Consider the effect of substituting 'large' for 'substantial' in the following examples:

> It is mandatory that candidates have experience of the control and motivation of a substantial work force[59]

> A substantial and well-diversified group of companies[60]

It is possible that in the first of these two instances 'substantial' means 'quite large' or 'not quite big enough to be called large', and in the second, 'well-established', 'adequately capitalised'. We are, however, deliberately left in a state of some confusion, which is always one of the prime objects of using jargon.

Americans dislike the name 'small car', although they may be enthusiastic about the advantages of such a vehicle. To meet this delicate situation, two euphemisms have been adopted. A car which is big by European standards, but small by American, is 'compact'. One which has the dimensions and the thirst of a European small car is 'subcompact', a very neat solution 'A subcompact rental car'.[61]

'Present' and 'continuous' are considered too static and accidental to describe anything which takes place in a modern, vigorous, growing, aggressive business. 'On-going' is the fashionable replacement. One company therefore seeks a recruit who 'will play a major part in the on-going profitable management and development of our business'.[62] Another announces that it attaches great importance to 'research to inform the on-going action'.[63]

'Maximise' is much used. There are those who insist that it does not mean merely 'make as big as possible', but 'make as profitably big as possible', which is not necessarily the same thing. The word is, however, so loosely used that one is never sure what meaning to attach to it in a particular context. 'Supported by a strong multi-discipline team, your principal objective will be to maximise the contribution to the operation, within a work environment which is constructive and positive'.[64]

There was a time when only carefully bred animals had pedigrees and this remains the correct use of the word. Business, disregarding this, uses 'pedigree' as a synonym for 'record', which raises considerations different from, and possibly more irreverent than those which the company probably had in mind. 'He came to Downsway with a good pedigree'[65] and 'Candidates should have a good product management pedigree'[66] both suggest that the people in question have been produced at a management breeding farm, which habitually wins the top prizes at a sort of managerial Crufts

Show. X is a top-class product manager because his father and mother were top-class product managers, and so back for generations.

After the Second World War a large number of ex-officers found their way into industry and commerce, in many cases with a considerable nostalgia for the golden years in uniform. Their military outlook may quite possibly be the cause of the introduction of 'report', instead of 'be responsible to', in such expressions as 'He will report to the Divisional Director'.[67]

'Report' contains the idea, as 'be responsible to' does not, of standing at attention and saluting briskly. It is an activity-word and, as such, certain to be well thought of in the business world, which finds the image, if not the reality, of constant movement flattering.

Among the intensifiers used to pump new life into tired old words, 'in-depth' has exceptional prestige. Firms will speak of an in-depth enquiry, instead of a thorough or careful enquiry, an in-depth report, instead of a detailed report. Quite often 'in-depth' means nothing at all, as in the demand for a management trainee with 'an in-depth determination to succeed'.[68]

Under the influence of business, useful words are changing their meaning with great speed. Not so long ago, hogshair came from pigs and had certain valuable characteristics as a result. Carpet tiles were made of it, but fell out of favour, because, like the pig himself, they needed regular watering to maintain them in good condition. Synthetic fibre therefore replaced the natural hogshair, leading to the advertising of 'A compressed fibre tile, using hogshair of manmade fibre'[69] which would seem to be pulling, if not the wool, then certainly the hogshair over the customer's eyes.

Business is subject to two quite different linguistic pressures. On the one hand there is the never-ending search for the new, even more arresting phrase, which will give a firm the edge over its rivals, and on the other, the wish to tone words down, to make them less dangerous, less precise, less likely to blow up in the face of the person who uses them. One's intentions can, of course, be frustrated if one's phrases should happen to fall into irreverent or unworthy hands. Take, for instance, 'the British hygiene-hire market'.[70] This, for those who are not well-informed on such matters, means 'the British towel-hire market', and one buys or hires towels in order to promote hygiene. One cannot hire hygiene, because anything which is hired has to be returned and it is difficult to see how this can be achieved with hygiene. 'Hygiene-hire' presumably came into existence as an up-to-date euphemism for 'towel-hire', which was felt to be rather low and old-fashioned. It made the whole business seem scientific and hospital-like and upgraded, at least theoretically, the firms which were engaged in it. To get the phrase accepted and known meant building up a high profile for it. Once this stage had been reached, 'hygiene-hire' could be allowed to have a low profile, like 'towel' itself. But immediately an irreverent outsider noticed it for the first time, laughed at it and singled it out for mention in a book it acquired a wholly unintended high profile again.

Business jargon is particularly susceptible to this kind of fate, largely because the business world takes itself so seriously and find nothing funny about the language it uses. Anyone with a strong sense of humour very rarely reaches the top levels of industry or commerce. Yet, looked at with a human pair of eyes a great deal of business jargon has great comic possibilities, a fact which is not well understood by those who create it and live with it.

Those outside the shoe industry, for instance, may well find it difficult not to show a little irreverence when they are presented with such ordinary pieces of in-house jargon as 'we are not growing in pairage output', and 'they were planning for an increase in pairage despatches in 1977'.[71]

One of the most extraordinary pieces of late twentieth-century jargon ever to appear was published in *The Times* in 1976.[72] It was a full-page, and therefore very expensive advertisement which contained almost every item of jargon of which the business world is capable. It summarises and points up everything that has been said and hinted at in the previous pages.

A promising start is made with the heading:

ARE YOU A WOMAN WITH THESE QUALITIES . . . . .

. . . . . Loyal
Capable of Open Communication
Intelligence, Integrity
A Person who Cares
Non Aggressive, Supportative
Excellent Personal Appearance
Social Skills, Excellent Grooming
Age 28-35, Disciplined
Career Need, Willing to Travel
Personal Need for Success
Adaptive, Resilient

The company, a financial consultancy, then explains itself and says why it needs this non-aggressive, supportative, intelligent, caring, adaptive, resilient woman.

> We are a professional money management organisation located in San Francisco, California. The president of our company – aged 38 – has been a financial professional for seventeen years and believes an administrative assistant/social secretary can make a significant contribution to his daily efforts.

The clients of our firm retain our services as investment counsel to manage their security portfolios on a professional fee basis. Our profession is a carriage trade profession and the clientele are typically well-educated affluent individuals. Our president has enjoyed excellent success in building a most unique professional money management organisation and the creative process is a major stimulus for him. It is enjoyable to him. We do not seek a business secretary as such. The candidate should ideally but is not required to possess, basic business skills, but, more importantly, be an individual prepared to accompany our president to client consultations where much privileged conversation is entrusted to a counsellor. The candidate should ideally be qualified to draft quantitative written reports of these meetings;

A client/counsellor relationship is one of growth predicated on trust. As the client/counsellor relationship grows over the years it is a natural progression for the counsellor – while visiting the client family – to be invited to participate in client family activities such as riding, swimming, attending ballet/symphony or a lecture. The candidate should be willing to participate and be comfortable in these activities. Secretaries are comparatively easy to locate, but women with poise, appearance, style – a finishing school type individual – are rare and valued by our president.

We are constructing a building near Palo Alto, California. Palo Alto is the home of Stanford University and many consider the area most attractive. Our building shall be totally private, self-sufficient and located in a natural wooded area. Our president is dedicated to a work environment which contributes to intellectual interaction; and is conducive to an enjoyable life style by our staff.

The candidate would ideally be single or divorced – with or without dependent children. Prerequisite qualities include an excellent memory, discretion regarding her knowledge of client estate matters and the ability to liaise graciously and effectively with business associates and clients. We shall strive to create an English home library work atmosphere. We anticipate an annual salary of $18,000 – $24,000 U.S. dollars exclusive of fringe benefits, which are excellent.

The position is structured to reward well a quite unique individual who honours a long-term career commitment. We shall endeavour to offer an unusual and, hopefully, stimulating intellectual and physical work environment coupled with a quite generous economic compensation package for a career employee.

If you are a perceptive, sensitive and intelligent individual capable of organising our president in a supportative manner and willing to become totally involved in all aspects of his professional life we invite you to forward a narrative letter, resume and, if possible, two photographs, to:

P.O. Box 2069, San Rafael, California 94902, U.S.A.

> Our executive recruitment consultant shall travel to England in the early Autumn, and the final selection shall be in November 1976, with employment effective January 1, 1977.

After reading this questions flood into the mind. Why was this Company advertising in Europe? Why was the home-bred American product not felt to be adequate to the task? What is an English home library work atmosphere? How exactly does one organise a president in a supportative manner? And, above all, what kind of paragon eventually got the job? It is interesting to notice that, among the many qualifications asked for, tolerance and a sense of humour do not appear.

This fact is a significant comment on the theme of the present book. Jargon is produced and used for the most part by humourless people who take themselves and their activities very seriously indeed and who need the jargon as a crutch to support them as they go about their work. In extreme cases the jargon is the man. Without it he hardly exists. With it, he stands some chance of appearing large and important, at least to those who take him at his face value.

Jargon is infectious. During the past four or five decades it has established itself with frightening strength among the kinds of people and occupations discussed in this book. It is now spreading out into other and previously unblighted fields. Museums, an international growth industry, are a case in point. They are a microcosm of what has been taking place more generally and what has been happening to them can be used as a dreadful warning.

The trouble here seems to have started in America. Americans, especially those of a scholarly turn of mind, find it almost impossible to be simple in public. Psychological and sociological jargon infects everything they write, as if plain English were evidence of a lack of education and, even worse, of a low income. The following passage illustrates the disease. It is part of a report on discussions between an American university and a local museum on the possibilities of sharing staff and the way in which this might be organised.

> A second conviction of the Committee is that the success of such a program of action is contingent not only upon the completeness of the administrative unit, but also upon a commitment to the requirements inherent in the kinds of activities its very existence will demand of faculty, referring specifically to the important problem of released faculty time required for instructional improvement.
>
> It is the further conviction of the Committee that if the administrative unit proposed is to be endowed at its inception with some inherent potential for success, then the Committee respectfully suggests that the two problems of faculty release time and the completeness of

the administrative unit and its implied functions must be considered as parallel and inseparable functions.

And so the Committee requested, not people and money so that it could get moving, but 'a commitment of personnel and monies to provide the organization necessary to initiate action', relying on an instinct which told it that it was more likely to get the money if it used the second kind of language rather than the first; that initiating action is altogether superior to getting moving. One must not blame the Americans too much for all this. Many of that country's linguistic abominations are no more than direct transfers of habits already well-established in Germany. The extract quoted above would translate with the greatest ease into German, a country in which official nonsense probably has an even higher prestige and certainly a longer pedigree than in the United States.

American museum literature does no more than follow the national trend. Its jargon and wordiness are no worse than one finds in any other kind of professional material, but to say that millions of people are suffering from the same disease does not make the disease any less serious. A brief anthology, from various American sources, will illustrate the problem and provide a background to the English examples to be discussed later. Nothing is lost by keeping them anonymous.

> Many museums seriously consider limiting ingress after the number of visitors inside reaches an optimum.

> . . . museums which are primarily profit-oriented as opposed to non-profit for tax-exempt purposes.

> . . . organizationally separate security responsibilities from professional museum responsibilities.

> The museum malady is certainly not a circulatory problem.

> Investigation grants from any private foundation, who giving guidelines can be possibly interpreted to include your museum operation.

> The City struggled back to financial stability in the late '30s, and resumed the role of maintenance support, but ceased appropriating funds for purchases.

> . . . the construction of a new museum facility.

> Nothing is more fundamental to a museum's operation than its assured fiscal future.

Anyone with the will to do so can prune, simplify and clean up this woolly, fraudulent English without too much difficulty. 'A new museum facility' is a new museum, 'primarily profit-oriented' means 'existing mainly to make money', and 'limiting ingress' means 'letting in no more visitors'. To discover any real meaning in 'a circulatory problem' needs more time and talent, however.

It is sad to discover good, vigorous people using the same dreadful language as the people who never had any creative spark in them at all, the mere administrators and time-servers. No museum in the world is less pompous or academic than the Brooklyn Children's Museum in New York, yet when a member of the staff – a very lively-minded person – was asked recently to produce a definition of 'museum', what emerged was 'a facility devoted to the preservation and promotion of the cultural arts and sciences through the use of specific resources that generally are not maintained in the course of daily events or used within the context of daily routine' – phrases which do not suggest the Brooklyn Children's Museum at all.

What is particularly clumsy and repulsive in the German-American habit – now spreading as fast in Britain as another recent import from North America, Dutch elm disease – of loading one's prose, quite unnecessarily, with compound nouns. A single page of an article from the *Curator*, which has its editorial base, one should note, in a museum staffed mainly by scientists, offered these examples: 'exhibit-design'; 'evaluation instruments'; 'design variables'; 'effectiveness variables'; 'exhibit effectiveness'; 'exhibit area'; 'exhibit presentation'; 'exhibit medium'; 'visitor ease'; 'head-count research'. And all this from a man with enough real feeling for the natural strength of American English to refer to 'the designer's temptation to use museum exhibits for the sizzle rather than the steak'.

These are undoubtedly people whose sensibilities have become so deadened by bureaucracy and pseudo-science that they can see and feel no difference between 'visitor ease' and 'making it easy and comfortable for visitors to see the exhibits', or between 'exhibit presentation' and 'the presentation of exhibits'. Any suggestion that 'head-count research' implies a curiously restricted and inhuman attitude towards one's fellow-beings is likely to be met with a look of incomprehension. And one does not make friends by pointing out the greyness and dullness and sheer bad writing of a passage such as this.

> In each of these areas, improved statements of intended objectives and evaluation instruments based on these objectives are of primary importance. Better statements of objectives and improved evaluation instruments can be prepared in the exhibit area. Ultimately, design variables can be related to effectiveness variables. Only when this is accomplished will it be possible to put the development of scientific and technical exhibits on a solid foundation.[73]

If museum staff think, speak and write in clichés there is a serious risk that museum visitors may do the same. Freshness and originality of response become less and less likely in an atmosphere conditioned by certain modern forms of 'professionalism'.

A study of the articles published during the past seven years in the British *Museums Journal* reveals very little of the worst forms of jargon. This may be, as one would like to think, because British museologists have not, as yet, been as disastrously corrupted as their American colleagues, or it may be because the *Museums Journal* has been conscientiously and ruthlessly edited, with the welfare of the profession and the nation always in mind. But there have been certain signs recently which give cause for disquiet. There is a good deal more 'label content' and 'label legibility' and a good deal less 'content of the labels' and 'legibility of the labels' than there used to be, although on nothing like the American scale, and nasty things like 'consumer preference schedules', 'production function', 'concomitant expansion in inputs', and 'spillover benefits' have been slipping through the editorial net from time to time to befoul otherwise interesting and well-written articles.

On the whole, the influence of the educational psychologists appears to be the most pernicious and insidious in Britain. Five years ago, this particular jargon-kind of writing was very rare in books and articles about museums by British authors. Now it is increasingly common. Here are two examples, both, one regrets to say, from the *Museums Journal*.

> Too many exhibits, or an imbalance between exhibits and labels might well have caused conceptual discontinuity and prevented the transfer to the long term memory of stimuli derived from the exhibit. Careful attention to the placing of the displays eased the intellectual selection and coding processes, and subtle cross-referencing of information appeared to assist the memory retrieval process.

This can be translated as: 'A well-planned and carefully-labelled exhibit helps the visitor to remember what he has seen'.

> A sequence of learning experiences was planned to accord with local school curricula, and also to sustain the more specific demands of the active speleologists.

These sentences are the machine-like and inelegant outpourings of a computer. They do not sound as if they have come from a human brain at all. 'We planned a sequence of learning experiences' is jargon, but it has some human quality about it. 'A sequence of learning experiences was planned' simply sounds like cold-blooded jargon, with no redeeming quality at all. It may well be that the reintroduction of 'I' and 'we' into contemporary museological writing would produce better written and therefore more readable articles. 'An exhibition was arranged' is a very dull, unarresting statement, compared with 'I arranged an exhibition'. The biggest crime of the scientists and the pseudo-scientists is that they have made the first person unfashionable and, in the process, widened the gap between written and spoken English to a dangerous extent. Every person caught writing a sentence like 'a sequence of learning experiences was planned to accord with local school curricula, and also to sustain the more specific demands of the active speleologists' should be compelled to read it aloud over and over again until every muscle in his body aches, and then to compose a translation into simple English, beginning with the word 'I' or, as a generous concession to modesty, 'we'.

Books Found Useful

A bibliography of writings on jargon would be extremely difficult, if not impossible to compile, partly because there is very little agreement as to what jargon is, and partly because the most significant comments tend to be an odd paragraph or sentence tucked away inside a book or article on a different subject.

All that can be attempted in the circumstances is therefore a list of the books which the author has found particularly useful during his researches into the subject. One's main reading for such a project is necessarily, however, in primary sources, that is, in the places where jargon is most likely to lurk. These have been indicated in footnotes to the text.

(A) *BOOKS ON THE CURRENT STATE OF ENGLISH*

Sir Ifor Evans (ed), *Studies in Communication* (London, 1957).

Sir Ernest Gowers, *ABC of Plain Words* (London, 1951).

Sir Ernest Gowers, *Plain Words: a Guide to the Use of English* (London, 1948).

Eric Partridge, *Usage and Abusage* (London, 1942).

Randolph Quirk, *The Use of English* (London, 1962).

T. A. Sebeok, *Style in Language* (New York, 1960).

P. D. Strevens, *The Study of the Present Day English Language* (Leeds, 1963).

J. Warburg, *The Best Chosen English* (London, 1957).

(B) *BOOKS ON THE SOCIAL CONTEXT OF ENGLISH*

A. M. Carr-Saunders and P. A. Wilson, *The Professions* (London, 1933).

F. R. Leavis and Denys Thompson, *Culture and Environment* (pub 1932).

George Orwell, *Critical Essays, Journalism and Letters*, ed. Sonia Orwell and Ian Angus (4 vols. London, 1967). Volume III is particularly valuable in this connection.

Lionel Trilling, *The Liberal Imagination* (London, 1951).

Raymond Williams, *Communications* (London, 1962).

Raymond Williams, *Culture and Society* (London, 1961).

(C) *BOOKS AND ARTICLES ON THE ENGLISH OF PARTICULAR PROFESSIONS AND OCCUPATIONS*

Louis Blom-Cooper, *The Language of the Law* (London, 1965).

Reginald O. Capp, *The Presentation of Technical Information* (London, 1973).

H. Evans, *Newsman's English* (London, 1972).

T. R. Henn, *Science in Writing* (London, 1960).

Lancelot Hogben, *The Vocabulary of Science* (London, 1953).

George Mandler and William Kessen, *The Language of Psychology* (New York, 1959).

H. Marcuse, *One Dimensional Man: Studies in the Ideology of Advanced Technology* (London, 1964).

Mary McCarthy, *Vietnam* (London, 1967).

F. A. Philbrick, *Language and the Law* (New York, 1949).

Ian T. Ramsey, *Religious Language* (London, 1957).

Glanville Williams, 'Language and the Law', *Law Quarterly Review*, (April 1945).

Peter Wright, *The Language of British Industry* (London, 1974).

Notes

INTRODUCTION

1. *Plain Words* (London: HMSO 1948) p. 6.
2. *ABC of Plain Words* (London: HMSO 1951) pp. 75-76.
3. *The Language of British Industry* (London: Macmillan, 1974) pp. 4-5
4. Cambridge *Reporter* (1959) p. 898. From a discussion in the Senate House, 4 March 1959.
5. March 1976.
6. Ibid. This forms part of an advertisement by a drug company. The advertisements in this and other American medical periodicals look and read like articles, which is, of course, the intention.
7. *British Medical Journal*, 23 July 1966.
8. *British Medical Journal*, advertisement, 2 July 1966.
9. *British Medical Journal*, 5th April 1975.
10. *American Journal of Psychiatry*, 128/2 (1971).
11. *American Journal of Psychiatry*, 128/2 (1971).
12. A. M. Carr-Saunders and P. A. Wilson, *The Professions*, (Oxford: Oxford University Press, 1933) pp. iii-iv.
13. Ibid., p. 3.
14. Ibid., pp. 3-4.
15. 14 April 1977.
16. 24 June 1955.
17. See also W. Lloyd Warner, *Social Class in America* (New York: Peter Smith, 1960). Mr Warner defines social class not only in terms of wealth and power but of the things that the members of any particular class spend their money on and the ways they spend their leisure.
18. *One Dimensional Man: Studies in the Ideology of Advanced Industrial Society* (London: Routledge, 1964) p. 88.
19. Ibid., p. 89.
20. *Vietnam* (New York: Harcourt, Brace, Jovanovich, and London: Weidenfeld and Nicolson, 1967). p. 18.
21. Ibid., p. 22.
22. Ibid., p. 47.
23. *Educational and Social Science*, 1/2 (July 1969).
24. *Sociology*, September 1975.
25. Zbigniew Brzezinski, 'America in the Technotronic Age', *Encounter*, January 1968.

26. William Michelson (ed)., *Behavioral Research Methods in Environmental Design* (Stroudsburg, Pa.: Hutchinson & Ross, Inc., 1975).
27. Karl H. Wörner, *Stockhausen,* Introduced, translated and edited by Bell Hopkins (London: Faber, 1973).
28. Milton Rokeach, *The Open and Closed Mind: Investigations Into the Nature of Belief Systems and Personality Systems* (New York: Basic Books, 1960).
29. *Journal of Educational Research*, 61/10 (July-August 1968).
30. *Educational and Social Science*, 1/2 (July 1969).
31. Daniel Solomon *et al., Teaching Styles and Learning* (Chicago: Center for the study of Liberal Education, 1963).
32. *Daily Telegraph* 5 February 1976.
33. *Sunday Times,* 20 June 1976.
34. *Daily Telegraph,* 1 July 1976.
35. *Daily Telegraph,* 23 January 1976.
36. John S. Brubacher, *Modern Philosophies of Education* (London: McGraw-Hill, 1969).
37. Seymour Martin Lipset, *Rebellion in the University* (Boston: Little, Brown & Co., 1971).
38. House of Commons Oral Answers, 5 February 1976.
39. Hedges & Butler's *Wine News,* August 1976.
40. *The Times,* 19 June 1976.
41. *Washington Star,* 17 October 1976.
42. *New Yorker*, 13 September 1976.
43. In *Allen v Thorn Electrical Industries, Ltd*, 1967.
44. *Words and Phrases Legally Defined* 2nd ed. (London: Butterworth, 1969).
45. In *Vaughan v Biggs,* 1960.
46. Quoted in Louis Blom-Cooper, *The Language of the Law* (London: The Bodley Head, 1965) p. 357.
47. R. B. Cattell, *The Description and Measurement of Personality* (World Books, 1946; Johnson Reprint, 1970).
48. *The Liberal Imagination* (London: Secker & Warburg, 1951).
49. The dangers of the situation are admirably outlined by C. P. Snow in *The Two Cultures and the Scientific Revolution,* (Cambridge: Cambridge University Press, 1959).
50. Reginald O. Kapp: *The Presentation of Technical Information* Constable, 1973).
51. *Nineteen Eighty Four* (London: Secker & Warburg, 1949).

CHAPTER 1

1. See A. Tindal Hart, *The Country Clergy in Elizabethan and Stuart Times,* (London Phoenix House, 1958), for an assessment of this during the first part of the reign of Queen Elizabeth I (pp. 24-6).

2. Sermon preached at the Court, 1634.
3. Preached 1694. Quoted here from 4th ed. of his works (1704) pp. 30-31.
4. Preached 1621. Quoted here from Nonesuch ed. of his works (1932) p. 602.
5. *Satires and Personal Writings*, ed. W. A. Eddy (Oxford: Oxford University Press, 1932) p. 274.
6. Quoted by F. P. Wilson, *Elizabethan and Jacobean*, (Oxford: Oxford University Press [Alexander Lecture, 1945]), pp. 4-5.
7. *The Summing-Up*, (London: Heinemann, 1952) p. 36.
8. *History of English Prose Rhythm* (1912) p. 158.
9. Professor C. H. Dodd, in an article in *The Observer*, 1 January 1961.
10. New Testament only (Oxford, 1961).
11. Prayer published for the Universal Day of Prayer for Students, 15 February 1953.
12. *Journal*, ed. Curnock, vol IV, (1909) p. 251
13. Ian Thomas Ramsey, *Religious Language* (London: SCM Press, 1957) p. 106.
14. On this, see Alex Comfort, *The Anxiety Makers*, (London: Panther Books, 1968).
15. *Uses and Abuses of Psychology* (London: Penguin, 1970) p. 15.
16. Ibid., p. 16.
17. *The Dynamics of Anxiety and Hysteria* (London: Routledge, 1957).
18. Joyce M. Watson, 'Glue-sniffing in profile', *The Practitioner*, vol. 218, no. 1304 (February 1977) p. 255.
19. Ibid., p. 258.
20. Karen E. Deveney and Lawrence W. Way, 'Effect of Different Absorbable Sutures on Healing of Gastrointestinal Anastomoses', *American Journal of Surgery*, January 1977. Papers from the 17th Annual Meeting of the Society for Surgery of the Alimentary Tract, Miami Beach, Florida.
21. Article by Ronald L. Weinsier *et al*, *American Journal of Medicine*, vol. 61 (December 1976).
22. Ibid., p. 815.
23. Ibid., p. 821.
24. D. J. Pallis and J. Birtchnell, 'Seriousness of Suicide Attempt in Relation to Personality', *British Journal of Psychiatry*, vol. 30 (March 1977) pp. 256-7.
25. *Salmond on the Law of Torts* 14th ed., ed. R. F. V. Heuston (London, 1965) p. 509.
26. Ibid., p. 478.
27. A. V. Dickey, *An Introduction to the Study of the Law of the Constitution*, 10th ed. (Macmillan, 1967).
28. *Allen v Thorn Electrical Industries, Ltd*, 1967.
29. 3rd ed., ed. Q. Hogg (London: Butterworth, 1961), vol. 36, p. 385.
30. *Bourne v Norwich Crematorium*, Ltd, 1967.
31. *Quinn v Associated Newspapers, Ltd*, 1967 (*Times Law Report*, 2

July 1957).

32. *Tolhurst v Webster*, 1936.
33. Ibid.
34. *Food and Drugs Act*, 1965, section 135 (1).
35. *Hairdressers' Registration Act*, 1964, section 15.
36. *Rex v Medical Appeal Tribunal, Ex parte Burpitt*, 1957.

CHAPTER 2

1. *Authority and Delinquency in the Modern State* (London: Routledge & Kegan Paul, 1950).
2. There is an ample supply of clues to this, e.g., 'I could think of few people more suitable than Willingdon for the BBC Chairmanship when, at the end of the year, it became vacant. I asked Lady Willingdon if he would like it; she was sure he would like it very much; what could she do? Willingdon told me later that, happening to meet the Prime Minister, his wife had broached the subject.' Lord Reith, *Into the Wind*, (London: Hodder & Stoughton, 1949), p. 256.
3. For a discussion of pressure-groups, see J. D. Stewart, *British Pressure Groups* (Oxford: Clarendon Press, 1958). 'Pressure groups,' he believes, 'are necessary to the government of our complex society. The coherent expression of opinion they render possible is vital. They have become a fifth estate, the means by which many individuals contribute to politics. Without them discontent would grow, and knowledge be lost.' (p. 244).
4. *British Political Parties* (London: Heinemann, 1955).
5. *The Spectator*, 8 February 1957.
6. 'Expressing the grievances of those with nothing to inherit or bequeath.' Michael Young, *The Rise of the Meritocracy*, (London: Thames and Hudson, 1958) p. 31. Young also points out (p.30) that this odd mixture within the Party caused 'the Morrises, Tawneys and Coles' to speak of 'the dignity of labour as though manual and mental work were of equal worth'.
7. p. 5.
8. On this, see Kenneth Hudson, 'The Last Chink in their Armour: the Metaphors of British Prime Ministers from Lloyd George to Harold Wilson', *Encounter*, March 1976.
9. *The Times*, 8 December 1962.
10. London: Weidenfeld & Nicolson, 1962, p. 189.
11. Fully reported and discussed in *The Times*, 11 March 1977.
12. For an interesting although now somewhat outdated glossary, see Mario Pei (ed.), *Language of the Specialists* (Funk and Wagnalls, 1966).
13. 39th ed., pp. 118-19.
14. T. Driberg, *The Listener*, 28 December 1950.

15. Commentary by Raymond Glendenning, 6 June 1950.
16. *Evening Standard* 18 June 1954. One should note in this connexion an anonymous leading article in *The Lancet*, 6 June 1959, demanding that action should be taken 'to end this evil'. 'The Medical case against boxing,' it says, 'is now so strong that as doctors we have a clear duty to fight for its total abolition. Any such move will have to contend with the very large financial interests concerned, with the strong and thoroughly unhealthy, though largely subconscious public appetite for violence and bloodshed, and with plain indifference.' (p. 1185). The article achieved absolutely nothing. Boxing is as powerfully entrenched as ever and the commentators and journalists are still able to feed the public hunger for blood, pain and injury.
17. *The Times*, 26 September 1950.
18. *The Spoil of Antwerp* (1576), quoted by A. T. Pollard, *An English Garner: Tudor Tracts, 1532–1588*, (1903), p. 444.
19. As Dr Ian Ramsey shrewdly put it, 'Through many years of Sir Winston Churchill's career it seemed to some of his critics that the love of phrases meant so much to him that he tended to judge causes by their rhetorical possibilities.' *Oratory and Literature* (Presidential Address to the English Association, 1960).
20. E. Partridge (ed.), *Dictionary of Forces' Slang, 1939-45* (London: Secker and Warburg, 1948).
21. *The Press*, (London: Penguin Special, 1938), p. 29.
22. For an excellent analysis of this, see Peter Evans, *Law and Disorder* (London: Secker and Warburg, 1956).
23. *Rationalism in Politics* (London: Methuen, 1962) p. 124.
24. *Left*, vol. 9, no. 2 (March 1977).
25. *Unemployment and the Crisis of Capitalism* (Labour Party, 1976).
26. Seymour Martin Lipset, *Rebellion in the University* (Boston: Little, Brown & Co., 1971).
27. Massimo Teodori (ed.), *The New Left: a Documentary History* (London: Bobbs-Merrill, 1970).
28. Seymour Martin Lipset, *op. cit.*
29. *Montreal Star*, 16 October 1976. Joe Morris, President of the Canadian Labour Congress.
30. C. Mullard, *Black Britain* (London: Inscape Corp., 1973). Reprinted 1975 under the title *On Being Black in Britain.*
31. *The Estate of Man* (London: Faber & Faber, 1951) p. 121.
32. John Strachey, *The Theory and Practice of Socialism* (London: Gollancz, 1938) p. 154.
33. pp. 60-1.

CHAPTER 3

1. Advertisement in *Sunday Telegraph*, 7 November 1976.
2. Advertisement in *Boston Sunday Globe*, 7 October 1976.
3. *New Yorker*, 27 December 1976. Advertisement by Charles Scribner's

Sons of W.A. Swanberg's book, *Norman Thomas. The Last Idealist.*
4. Ibid. Advertisement of *Dawns + Dusks*, by Louise Nevelson.
5. *The Times*, 7 August 1976.
6. *Critical Quarterly*, Autumn 1960. Advertisement for Goronowy Rees' book, *A Bundle of Sensations.* The quotation is taken from a review Connolly wrote for the *Sunday Times.*
7. *Critical Essays, Journalism and Letters of George Orwell*, ed. Sonia Orwell and Ian Angus, vol. III, pp. 168-9 (London: Secker & Warburg, 1968).
8. Ibid., vol. IV, p. 182.
9. Ibid., vol. III, p. 311.
10. *Culture and Society, 1780-1950* (London: Chatto & Windus 1959) p. 199.
11. Ibid., p. 257.
12. Ibid., p. 295.
13. A.R. Jones, 'The Theatre of Arnold Wesker', *Critical Quarterly*, Winter 1960, p. 367.
14. Ibid., p. 367.
15. Ibid., p. 366 (Italics added).
16. Vol. 163 (September/December 1966).
17. Ibid.
18. John Berger and others, *The Art of Seeing* (BBC/Penguin Books, 1972) p.10.
19. Ibid., p. 11.
20. Ibid., p. 11.
21. From a review of Peter Conrad, *Landseer: The Victorian Paragon* (1976), in the *Observer*, 30 May 1976.
22. Roland Penrose, *Picasso* (London: Pelican Books, 1971) p. 141.
23. Eric Salzman: *Twentieth Century Music: An Introduction* (New Jersey: Prentice-Hall, 2nd ed., 1974) p. 22.
24. *Musical Quarterly* (New York) April 1976. Record review by Robert Moeus.
25. Karl H. Wörner, *Stockhausen.* Introduced, translated and edited by Bell Hopkins (London: Faber, 1973) p. 62.
26. Ibid., p. 79.
27. Eric Salzman, *op. cit.* p. 35.
28. Ibid., p. 113.
29. Ibid., p. 162.
30. Ibid., p. 188.
31. Stanley Sadie, *The Times*, 30 October 1976.
32. Thomas Clifton, 'The Poetics of Musical Silence', in *Musical Quarterly* (New York) April 1976.
33. *Classical Music*, 20 October 1976.
34. *The Times*, 16 October 1976.
35. *Financial Times*, 7 December 1976.
36. Review by Bruce Morrison, *Music and Musicians*, August 1976.

37. Review by Robert Maycock, *Music and Musicians*, August 1976.
38. *Classical Music*, 20 October 1976, referring to a performance of Tchaikovsky's Fourth Symphony.
39. Interview with the composer, Alberto Ginastera, *Classical Music*, 20 October 1976.
40. *Financial Times*, 18 November 1976.
41. *Music and Musicians*, August 1976. Review, by Robert Fink and Robert Ricci, of *The Language of Modern Music*.
42. Andy Grunberg, 'Photography, Chicago, Moholy and After', *Art in America*, September/October 1976.
43. Article by Walter Klepac on Pierre Boogaert, *Arts Canada*, July/August 1976.
44. John Russell and Suzi Gablik (eds.), *Pop Art Redefined* (London: Thames and Hudson, 1969) p. 54.
45. Ibid., p. 12.
46. Ibid., p. 13.
47. John H. Walker, *Art Since Pop*, (London: Thames and Hudson, 1975) pp. 6-7.
48. *The Times*, 16 October 1976.
49. Review by Richard Gilbert of Richard Boston's book, *Beer and Skittles*, in *The Listener*, 5 August 1976.
50. An obituary notice on André Simon, quoting a speech made by Charles Morgan at the Saintsbury Club in 1947, 'in which he poked fun at the cellarer's spoken and written style'. From *Number Three* (the magazine of Berry Bros and Rudd) Autumn 1975.
51. Trust House Forte menu, Coventry, February 1976.
52. Howard Johnson menu, Dallas, Texas, 1973.
53. Ibid.
54. Menu of Merrimack Valley Motor Inn, Massachusetts, 1974.
55. Ibid.
56. *New Yorker*, 22 December 1975.
57. Trust House Forte menu, Coventry, February 1976.
58. *The 4th Estate* (Halifax, Nova Scotia) October 1976.
59. *High Life* (British Airways' in-flight magazine) October 1976.
60. Swallow Hotels brochure.

CHAPTER 4

1. A. Street and W. Alexander: *Metals in the Service of Man* (London: Penguin, 1944) p. 39.
2. Quoted by Lionel Trilling in *The Liberal Imagination* (London: Secker & Warberg, 1951) p. 285.
3. George C. Hemmens, *The Structure of Urban Activity Linkages* (North Carolina: Center for Urban and Regional Studies, Institute for Reasearch in Social Science, Chapel Hill, 1966) pp. 5-6.

4. *British Journal of Sociology*, March 1968.
5. Robert M Marsh: *Comparative Sociology: a Codification of Cross-Societal Analysis* (Harcourt Brace, 1971) p. 141.
6. Ibid., p. 158.
7. *Sociology*, September 1975.
8. David Lowenthal and Marquita Riel, *Environmental Structures; Semantic and Experimental Components* (American Geographical Society, 1972) p. 42.
9. Ronald A. Hoppe *et al., Early Experiences and the Process of Socialisation* (New York, 1970) p. 82.
10. Alvin W. Gouldner, *The Coming Crisis of Western Sociology* (London: Heinemann, 1971) pp. 47-8.
11. Ibid., p. 51.
12. Ibid., p. 56.
13. On this problem, see Mario Pei (ed.), *Language of the Specialists* (Funk and Wagnalls, 1966). This book points out the difficulties caused by what it calls 'overlapping terminology', which means that 'different sociologists may use different terms to mean substantially the same thing, or they may have a somewhat different definition disciplines, e.g. anthropology, economics and sociology, use the same word, such as 'culture' or 'value' in different ways. The conclusion is that 'the existence of overlapping terminology reflects the fact that sociology is still a young field which has not yet completely codified its terminology'. (p. 124)
14. Paul F. Lazarfeld *et al., Continuities in the Language of Social Research* (New York: The Free Press, 1972) p.2.
15. Richard Swinburne, *An Introduction to Confirmation Theory* (London: Methuen, 1973) pp. 113-14.
16. Ibid., pp. 113-14.
17. Ibid., p. 73.
18. *Journal of Educational Psychology*, vol. 61, no. 3 (1970).
19. *Journal of Educational Research*, vol. 60, no. 3 (November 1966).
20. *Journal of Educational Research*, vol. 61, no. 8 (April 1968).
21. *Journal of Educational Research*, vol. 60, no. 5 (January 1967).
22. *Journal of Educational Research*, vol. 61, no. 8 (April 1968).
23. *Journal of Educational Psychology*, vol. 61, no. 2 (1970).
24. *Journal of Educational Psychology*, vol. 62, no. 1 (February 1971).
25. *Journal of Educational Psychology*, vol. 59, no. 1 (1968).
26. *Journal of Educational Psychology*, vol. 64. no. 1 (1873).
27. *Journal of Educational Research*, vol. 61, no. 10 (July/August 1968).
28. *Journal of Educational Research*, vol. 61, no. 8 (April 1968).
29. *Journal of Educational Psychology*, vol. 61, no. 1 (1970).
30. The point is well discussed in Benjamin S. Bloom, *Taxonomy of Educational Objectivity*, Book 1: *Cognitive Domain* (Longman, 1972, 17th impression) It is worth recording that, despite its forbidding title, this book contains practically no jargon at all, a miraculous achievement.

31. Daniel Solomon *et al.*, *Teaching Styles and Learning* (Chicago: Center for the Study of Liberal Education for Adults, 1963) pp. 22-3.
32. Ibid., p. 57.
33. Ibid., p. 75.
34. Ibid., p. 101.
35. Ibid., p. 102.
36. J.M. Perreault, *Towards a Theory for UDC* (London: Clive Bingley, 1969).
37. Neil Friedman, *The Social Nature of Psychological Research* (New York: Basic Books, 1967) p. 161.
38. *Technology and Economic Development* (New York, 1963).
39. G.L. Shackle, *Decision, Order and Time in Human Affairs* (Cambridge: Cambridge University Press, 1961) pp. 219-20.
40. Steven A.Y. Lin, *Theory and Measurement of Economic Externalities* (New York: Academic Press, 1967) pp. 150-1.
41. Ibid., pp. 188-9.

CHAPTER 5

1. Henry Sampson, *History of Advertising* (London: John Murray, 1874) p. 556.
2. H.G. Lazell (Beecham Group), reported in *The Times*, 30 July 1959.
3. The British estate-agents' traditional style may become somewhat cramped as a result of the recommendation of the Director of Fair Trading, in 1976, that the Trades Description Act 1968 should be extended to cover the sale of property. It was put to the Director-General that the public is 'accustomed to a modest degree of hyperbole' in estate-agents' advertisements, but the argument failed to impress him.
4. E.H. Brooks and Son.
5. *Sunday Times*, 22 January 1961.
6. *Sunday Times*, 8 January 1961.
7. *New Yorker*, 13 December 1975.
8. *New Yorker*, 8 November 1976.
9. Advertisement by Carras, New York, *New Yorker*, 14 June 1976.
10. *The Hidden Persuaders* (Longmans, 1957) p. 100.
11. Advertisement in the *New Yorker*, 27 September 1976.
12. *English in Advertising: a linguistic study of advertising in Great Britain* (Longmans, 1966).
13. Ibid., p. 156.
14. Ibid., p. 150.
15. *London Recorder*, 5 September, 1790.
16. *Observer*, 12 February 1961.
17. *Sunday Telegraph*, 10 April 1977.
18. *Illustrated London News*, July 1976.
19. *Sunday Telegraph* Magazine, 19 March 1977.

20. *Woodies interprets fall '76 interiors* (brochure of Woods and Taylors store), Washington DC, 1976.
21. *The Garden* (Journal of the Royal Horticultural Society) April 1977.
22. *Financial Times*, 17 April 1976.
23. Advertisement by Lamson Industries, *Daily Telegraph*, 27 November 1975.
24. *Daily Telegraph*, 27 November 1975.
25. The John Lewis Partnership achieves distinction by using the simple, old-fashioned word 'pay', when all its competitors refer to 'remuneration', 'emoluments' and the other mealy-mouthed expressions. 'Senior Personnel Appointment . . . Pay will be in the range of £4,250-£5,250.'
26. *Daily Telegraph*, 29 April 1976. The *Telegraph*, with its large number of advertisements for managerial posts, is a particularly good hunting-ground for this kind of jargon.
27. *The Times*, 30 May 1976.
28. *Daily Telegraph*, 28 September 1976.
29. *Daily Telegraph*, 17 September 1976.
30. *The Times*, 5 April 1977.
31. *Daily Telegraph*, 5 February 1976.
32. *New Society*, 4 December 1976.
33. *Daily Telegraph*, 30 April 1976.
34. 'Industry' is used here in the wider sense of manufacturing, commerce and transport.
35. *Daily Telegraph*, 23 January 1976.
36. *Daily Telegraph*, 27 November 1975.
37. *Sunday Times*, 30 November 1975.
38. *Daily Telegraph*, 6 February 1976.
39. *Daily Telegraph*, 17 December 1976.
40. *Daily Telegraph*, 22 January 1976.
41. *Daily Telegraph*, 9 December 1975.
42. Ministry of Defence. The use of the initials is jargon in its own right.
43. *Daily Telegraph*, 27 February 1976.
44. *Times Higher Education Supplement*, 13 February 1976.
45. *Boston Sunday Globe*, 10 October 1976.
46. Brochure of Royal County Hotel, Durham, 1976.
47. *The Age*, Melbourne, Australia, 28 February 1960.
48. *Boston Sunday Globe*, 10 October 1976.
49. *Delta Flightline Catalogue*, 1976.
50. *Daily Telegraph*, 27 November 1975.
51. *Sunday Times*, 30 November 1975.
52. *The Sun* (Australia) 2 March 1976.
53. *Boston Sunday Globe*, 10 October 1976.
54. Ibid.
55. *Daily Telegraph*, 27 November 1975.
56. Ibid.
57. *New Yorker*, 1 October 1975.
58. *Sunday Times*, 15 November 1975.

59. *Sunday Times.* 30 May 1976.
60. *The Age*, Melbourne, Australia, 20 March 1976.
61. *New York Times*, 12 October 1976.
62. *Daily Telegraph*, 5 February 1976.
63. *New Society*, 4 December 1975.
64. *Sunday Times*, 20 June 1976.
65. *Financial Times*, 14 January 1976.
66. *Daily Telegraph*, 27 November 1975.
67. *Daily Telegraph*, 5 December 1975.
68. *Daily Telegraph*, 12 February 1976.
69. *Business and Finance*, Dublin, 8 April 1976.
70. *Daily Telegraph*, 17 December 1975.
71. Lance Clark, Managing Director of C. and J. Clark, quoted in *Shepton Mallet Gazette*, 14 April 1977.
72. *The Times*, 22 July 1976.

Index